Women Leaders In Ministry

From Bondage To Freedom At Last!

Women Leaders In Ministry

From Bondage To Freedom At Last!

Myrtle Pellew

Copyright © 2011 by Myrtle Pellew.

Library of Congress Control Number: 2011919184
ISBN: Hardcover   978-1-4653-8688-5
             Softcover   978-1-4653-8687-8
             Ebook   978-1-4653-8689-2

All rights reserved. No part of this book may be reproduced or transmitted in any form or by any means, electronic or mechanical, including photocopying, recording, or by any information storage and retrieval system, without permission in writing from the copyright owner.

This book was printed in the United States of America.

To order additional copies of this book, contact:
Xlibris Corporation
1-888-795-4274
www.Xlibris.com
Orders@Xlibris.com

This book is dedicated to women leaders in ministry who have gone before, those who are and those who are to come, as well as to men throughout the ages who have supported and will continue to support women leaders in their quest for freedom.

Table of Contents

Preface xi
Foreword xiii
Acknowledgements xv
Introduction xvii
Chapter 1: Historical Perspectives on the Subordination of Women 1
    Meaning of Subordination 1
    Godly Subordination versus Ungodly Subordination 2
    Principle of Subordination in Ministry 4
    The Subordination Myth 5
    Arguments for and against the Subordination of Women 8
    The Fall and Its Consequences 10
    Inferiority Myth 12
        Biological Inferiority 13
        Intellectual Inferiority 13
        Social Inferiority 14
        Spiritual Inferiority 14
    Early Christian Attitudes toward Women 15
    Jesus Christ and Women 17
    Paul and Women 20
    Patriarchy in the Church 22
Chapter 2: Leadership—Authority, Power, and Submission 29
    Authority 32
    Paul and the Use of Authority 34
    Teaching and Authority 34
    Authority in Today's Context 37

- Authoritative Concept of Office in the New Testament in the Post-Pauline Church and in the Present-Day Church 38
- The Meaning of *Headship* and Authority in Paul's Writings 40
- Power 44
  - Good and Evil Use of Power 44
- Submission 47
  - The Dominance and Submission Model 48
  - The Mutual Submissive Model 50
- Chapter 3: Women Leaders in Old and New Testament Times 55
- Women Leaders in the Old Testament 55
- Women as Leaders in the Hebrew Community 57
  - Prophetesses 57
    - Miriam 57
    - Deborah 58
    - Huldah 59
    - Unnamed Woman Prophet 59
    - Other Influential Women 59
    - Hebrew Queens 60
- Women Leaders in the New Testament 60
- Women Leaders in the Apostolic Church 61
  - Phoebe 63
  - Junia 63
  - Euodia and Syntyche 63
  - The Other Women 64
- Women Leaders in the Pastoral Epistles and Post-Pauline Church 64
  - The Elect Lady 64
  - Women Presbyters 65
  - The Order of Widows 65
  - Women Deacons 66
  - The Decline of Deaconesses 68
- Chapter 4: The Question of Ordination 71
- The Meaning and Purpose of Ordination 71
- The Ordained Office in the Church 72
  - Ordination—The Ordained of Today 73
  - Spiritual Gifts and the Ordained Office 74
  - Ordination of Women and New Testament Principles 75
  - Women Ordination—A Radical Departure from the Traditional Roles 77

    Opposing Views Regarding the Ordination of Women 78
Positions of Various Denominations on the Question of
    Ordination of Women 81
        The Methodist Church 84
        The Presbyterian Church...85
        The Lutheran Church..85
        The Church of England...85
        The Orthodox and Roman Catholic Churches............................87
        Freewill Baptists...88
        The Southern Baptist Convention 88
        The North American Baptist Conference 88
        The Conservative Baptist Association..88
Chapter 5: Women Leaders in Contemporary Times 91
    Nineteenth Century Conservative Reaction 92
    Contributions of Women Leaders as Pioneers 93
    Women Preachers of the Nineteenth and Twentieth Centuries 95
    Women Leaders of the Twentieth Century 98
    Pioneers of the Pentecostal Movement 98
    Women Leaders of the Twenty-First Century................................. 100
    Women Leaders in Missions in the Nineteenth and Twentieth
        Centuries 102
        Women's Movements...102
        Examples of Women Leaders in Missionary Activities 104
        Contemporary Women's Movements..107
Chapter 6: Marginalization and Struggles of Women Leaders in
        Ministry...113
    Marginalization and Early Christian Offices for Women...................113
    Historical Perspectives on Discrimination against Women 115
        Perceived Sexist Discrimination against Women.......................119
        Traditional Roles 119
        Salary...119
        Single versus Married 120
        Job Shortages... 120
        Verbal and Sexual Harassment... 120
        Coping Strategies of Women Against Harassment 121
        Three Phases of Marginalization 122
        Issues of Invisibility and Silence...123

  Subordinate Positions for Female Pastors in Relation to Male
    Pastors... 124
  Twentieth-Century Conferences and Movements to Address
    the Struggles..125
Chapter 7: Leadership Styles of Women.. 129
  Church Women and Their Style of Leadership.................................... 129
  Paradigm of Woman Leadership...131
  Locus of Leadership Power 133
  Partnership Style and Stress in Leadership... 134
Conclusion: Beyond the Present—A New Approach to Ministry............137
  Charismatic and Administrative Components of the Church 137
  Servanthood in Ministry 138
  Effects of the Fall on Man and Woman Relationships 140
  Impact of the Effects of the Fall on the New Creation 141
  A Reflection on Early Christianity..142
  The Church as a Liberation Community..143
  Ministry as Mutual Empowerment of the New Community..............144
  The Future of Women in Ministry..145
  Solution of Women Leaders' Problem 146
Bibliography 151
Index... 161
Testimonials 169

Preface

I am very happy to endorse the timely book *Women Leaders in Ministry: From Bondage to Freedom at Last!* written by Dr. Myrtle Pellew. This subject confronts us in our everyday lives, be it in the classroom, in our personal lives, in all of our relationships and social lives.

Women have come through a long struggle with the devil's wiles in such areas as overcoming aggression and violence, and making lifestyle choices that have worked against their true spiritual roots. Women are eternal mothers, daughters, sisters, wives and the gender that keeps us connected to the key seeds of intimacy, passion, drama and psyche. The feminine soul cries out for heart connection and for re-awakening to man's hard wired knowledge that is death to the heart.

The author has done a magnificent job at awakening us to a thorough and practical history and handbook for a sex that has been wounded and hindered by its past, resulting in a misunderstanding of the ways of the Lord.

Dr. Stephen Hambly, Ph.D, D-CPC
Dean of Psychology in Counselling at
Canadian Christian Counsellors College
Vice-President, International Development at
California State Christian University

Foreword:

This book *Women Leaders in Ministry: From Bondage to Freedom at Last!* is an exhaustive, scripturally based work that is geared towards encouraging and empowering women during these last days so that they can use their giftings to bless their local churches and to impact the larger society. If you are a pastor or are in full time ministry, this book will give you the confidence to release the females who have the five-fold ministry gifts in your church to labor in God's vineyard.

    This book is well-written, historically accurate, and scripturally based. I recommend that it should be read by anyone in ministry. It will provide those who read it with clarity to their call and to how God sees them.

Pastor Marcus Martinez
Senior Pastor, Destiny and Dominion Word Ministries.

Acknowledgements:

In order to produce this book of such a nature and magnitude successfully, I owe debts of gratitude to several people who have been instrumental in contributing towards making the publication of this book a reality. Above all, I give praise, thanks, glory and honor to the Holy Spirit for giving me a title for this book and for instructing me to publish it, as well as for His illumination, inspiration and guidance throughout its production. I wish to express my deepest appreciation to my senior pastor, Marcus Martinez for his kind assistance, valuable input and critique towards the success of this book. I am truly indebted to Dr. Stephen Hambly for his insight and neutrality on a controversial topic and for his timely comments. I extend my sincere thanks to Reverend Gord Constantine, a friend and mentor of many years for his words of encouragement and his candid perspective about the roles and functions of women in ministry. I am deeply grateful to my dear friends and sisters in Christ, Reverend Janet Thompson, Waveney Job, Barbara Cain and Joylyn Hewitt for taking time to read the manuscript, for their kind support and constructive comments by which I am truly humbled. Lastly, I salute my beloved family whose words of wisdom, constructive advice, patience and cooperation have been remarkable and very highly appreciated.

May God's richest blessings be yours!

Myrtle Pellew

Introduction

For centuries, the controversy surrounding women leaders in ministry has prevailed globally in various Christian denominations. Beneath this controversy, there is an undercurrent of schism, deep-rooted dissatisfaction and frustration, lack of freedom, marginalization, and oppression in the body of Christ. Such great emphasis is placed on the traditions of men and rigid man-made barriers, that made it extremely difficult, if not virtually impossible, for women leaders to attain great heights in ministry. Women must endure this struggle in order to be active participants in the ministry and mission that Jesus Christ imparted to His body.

Embedded in this milieu of controversy are adversarial and contending positions and various schools of thought to support or refute the leadership of women in ministry. Such positions reflect antiquated or modernized viewpoints, spanning the dawn of creation to the present-day church. Over the centuries, women have struggled to carve a genuine identity for themselves in ministry as negative attitudes toward women leaders persist. Women are clamoring to be heard and are made to feel like second-class citizens of heaven. The following are some crucial questions that need to be addressed: Should women minister in the church? Should they assume various leadership positions or roles in ministry? Is there any justification for prohibiting women ministers from exercising authority over men in the body of Christ? Should women leaders be restricted to certain areas of ministry?

It is a given fact that men and women are called to minister upon their identification with Jesus Christ in water baptism and that they are empowered by the Holy Spirit to perform this ministry. However, the issue of women assuming leadership roles in ministry has always been a hot topic for debate.

The author believes that women can be chosen, equipped, and ordained by God to assume various leadership positions in ministry. Women should not be restricted from participating fully in the body of Christ because of social and cultural barriers, societal norms, the male dominance theory, and the patriarchal and hierarchical structure in society and in the church. In addition, some church denominations prohibit women from assuming some ministerial positions due to sex, gender, or race.

On the matter of authority, an existing predominant view is that God ordained female subordination to male authority. As a result, women leaders may be expected to perform supportive roles in ministry to male leaders and may therefore be subjected to the painful effects of marginalization as they are placed in secondary roles. It must be noted that leadership, authority, and power are inextricably linked and that these three concepts must be viewed in the context of servanthood for those who participate in ministry. As head of the church, Jesus Christ invests authority and power in both male and female to carry out the Great Commission to go and teach all nations, baptizing them in the name of the Father and of the Son and of the Holy Ghost (Matthew 28:19). Walking in the footsteps of Jesus Christ, the humblest of servants that ever lived, leaders must be aware that their greatest function is to serve. Authority and power must not be exercised to control others. Both male and female leaders should serve in humility, considering the fact that God resists the proud but gives grace to the humble (1 Peter 5:5). Therefore, women leaders should not lord it over others or be made to feel that they are doing so by their male counterparts.

Women leaders in ministry have struggled long and hard to take their rightful places in ministry. Even though they have labored alongside men in ministry from the inception of the church, their spiritual and social statuses have been devalued although they have proven in some cases to be just as capable as or even more capable than men in performing certain leadership tasks. For example, on the mission field, women have pioneered many missionary activities but have been required to subsequently hand them over to male leadership.

Women have always served in leadership roles in both the secular and spiritual realms. In the spiritual realm, God the Holy Spirit bestows gifts on whom He wills. Therefore, there is no justification for humans to limit God or to limit women leaders in ministry. The walls created by a male-dominated, hierarchical structure in the church should be broken down so that women could exercise freedom in Christ. Women need freedom to perform their leadership roles and to realize their identity in God. Only then would the church experience equality and mutuality in God.

This book is written to energize and mobilize women leaders in ministry to pursue and hold fast to the ministry God has called them to and for the church to embrace the necessity to permit equal opportunities of service for men and women leaders by creating a healthy work environment in the body of Christ. Women leaders should rest assured that the sole criterion for determining their ministerial role is the call of God on their lives and should be emboldened to heed this call. The church was born to liberate women from its man-made structures, to enjoy total freedom to serve in its charismatic framework.

Chapter One:
Historical Perspectives on the Subordination of Women

In an effort to examine historical perspectives on the subordination of women, three words are commonly used interchangeably. These words are *subordination*, *subservience*, and *submission*. In the secular realm, submission may not necessarily be equated with subordination but may be viewed as a positive component of subordination that bears a negative connotation. A person who submits to another person does so with the right to choose, a degree of willingness, and an element of trust. Submission speaks of availability of oneself, commitment to another's discretion, obedience, meekness, and humility, which are crucial elements and virtues in the lives of Christians who must not only submit or yield to the power and authority of the Almighty God but to the power and authority of one another as well.

Meaning of Subordination

Subordination may be defined as a divinely given principle that predates both Christianity and Judaism, as well as custom and culture. God instituted this principle at the dawn of patriarchy, in the Garden of Eden, by placing woman in subordination to man. Genesis 3:16 states that a husband is to rule over his wife.[1]

Godly Subordination versus Ungodly Subordination

The biblical principle of subordination depicts a voluntary union between God the Father and God the Son, between man and Christ, and between man and woman. God the Father is the head of Jesus Christ, who lived His entire life in submission to His Father in order to complete the plan of salvation. Man is subordinate to Christ who is head of the universal church, King of kings, and Lord of lords. Another aspect of this principle states that woman is subordinate to man. By submitting Himself to His Father, Jesus Christ gained a position of authority and power. Man can be fulfilled by subjecting himself to Jesus Christ's authority. Likewise, a woman is fulfilled by being subordinate to her husband.[2] In her subordination, she is endowed with authority because she is her husband's helper and because she and her husband are mutually dependent on each other. Godly subordination is in order when it does not involve male dictatorship and complies with the godly principle of subordination.

God the Creator is the final source of all power and authority. The three persons of the Godhead are not dictators and do not impose Their will on anyone. However, we are obligated to be subordinate to God's authority. We must place ourselves under His divine control and will in which there is no inkling of inferiority, bondage, or lack of freedom. We must stand in awe of a majestic, omniscient, omnipotent, and omnipresent God who has made us free moral agents to choose to make Him Lord of our lives. We must bow in adoration to His authority as we place our faith, will, and understanding in subordination to His will and understanding for our lives. It is sinful and a crime for humans to be insubordinate to God and to His word.

Although *subordination* is a functional and positional word like *submission*, ungodly subordination bears a negative connotation that implies control, inferiority, servility, bondage, rendering of service in another's interest, and lack of freedom to choose. Outside of God, humans have the tendency to gravitate toward dictatorship. In the case of women, several arguments have been put forward for and against their subordination, dating back to creation. In support of the creation theory is the spiritual inferiority argument that views women as both inferior and unequal to men. In the ancient world, the subordination of women was mainly dependent on the cultural milieu and societal norms of those times. With the dawn of the Christian era, a shift in this paradigm became evident as the pendulum swung in favor of spiritual equality in Christ. However, church history is fraught with the ungodly subordination of women due to the presence of patriarchy and the hierarchical structure of the church. In the present-day church, the principle of male dominance continues to hold sway over the leadership roles of women in ministry, subjecting women to subordinate positions. The church has mistreated women leaders over the centuries even though the Bible does not condone male dictatorship. Women leaders are struggling to take their rightful places in the ministry and in the body of Christ and need to be empowered to do so.

Man and woman were created equal in the image of God. They are intended to serve God as equals, but the capacities under which they serve in the body of Christ are under close scrutiny. Some opponents of women leadership have argued that women should always be subordinate to male leadership. This subordination implies that women leaders' status and position in ministry must be in subjection to male leadership. Thus, subordination serves as a form of oppression as it compromises the freedom of women to function in ministry.

There is no comparable analogy between the submission of Jesus Christ to God the Father in the divine plan of salvation and the subordination of women leaders to male leadership in ministry. The three persons of the Godhead are one and the same in essence, but their functional roles are different. Jesus Christ confirmed that He and the Father are one (John 10:30). Thomas Schriener lent clarity to this functional role by pointing out that the Son is not essentially inferior to the Father, but that He willingly submitted Himself to His Father's authority.[3] There is no ontological difference between the Father and the Son.

In the Doctrine of the Trinity, Lockyer shed light on the divine nature of God by noting that the Nicene Creed of AD 325 pointed out that the Trinity consists of three divine persons with one substance. He cited W. P. Pope, a renowned theologian, said that the Trinity is "one divine Essence [which] exists in a Trinity of coequal personal subsistence, related as the Father, the Eternal Son of the Father, and the Holy Ghost eternally proceeding from the Father."[4] Lockyer identified the separate function of God the Father as "the Great Upholder and Purpose of all things" and of God the Son as "the One and Only Redeemer of Mankind" and of the Holy Ghost as "the Indispensable Sanctifier and Enlightener."[5]

The coequality, coexistence, and codependence of the Father and the Son, though unique, depict a valuable example of how Jesus Christ requires the relationship between man and woman in His body to operate, thus confirming the full and equal partnership of man and woman in ministry. Inherent in Jesus Christ's willing submission to His Father is mutual respect between the Father and the Son, with no inkling of coercion or control. Jesus Christ's temporary submission to His Father in drawing salvation's plan does not necessitate ontological subordination and does not justify the subordination of woman to man to address the gender issue of subordination.

In his examination and analysis of spiritual equality and societal subordination, Longenecker stressed the fact that, although society requires order when some people function as overseers and others as subordinates, this does not conclude that one gender must function as overseer and the other as subordinate. He also pointed out the difficulty of speaking about subordination of status without implying the inferiority of a person,[6] which is contradictory to spiritual equality in Christ.

Principle of Subordination in Ministry

The principle of subordination is universal. As Jesus Christ was subordinate to His father, so everyone is subordinate to someone else. In his discussion of the biblical principle of subordination, Melick identified economic subordination and organizational subordination. He noted that equality in the Godhead is similar to equality among humans. The three persons of the Godhead share deity and the common mission of redemption. Humans share the same values, the capacity for companionship and cooperation in specific tasks. Economic subordination is the activity of God in which the three persons of the Godhead have a division of labor. They focus on the two primary tasks of creation and redemption. Their model of equality and economic subordination is to be emulated by both the family and the church.

In organizational subordination, equality is the key. Each person must recognize and appreciate essential equality and value the worth of another. Communication and love are to characterize internal relationship, and each person is to focus jointly on the task. As a result, no jealousy, strife, contention, or claims of superiority or inferiority will exist.[7]

However, it is crucial to remember that, in the context of ministry, subordination does not imply inferiority if the biblical principle of spiritual equality is to stand firm. The will of God reveals that there is a distinct difference between a man and a woman. This difference is mainly functional in nature. Although functionally subordinate to a man, a woman is by no means inferior to man. The Bible declares that God is the Head of Christ, but

Christ is not inferior to His father. He willingly submitted Himself to His father's authority to complete the work of salvation. This principle applies to the man-woman relationship in the affairs of daily living in which man assumes the executive position.

Functionally, this pattern is applicable in ministry as long as there are men who are anointed by God to assume this position. It is fair to say that in some situations, normal circumstances may be superseded by abnormal practices and extraordinary conditions.[8] For example, women are sometimes forced to assume executive positions on the mission field in the absence of men.[9] Another example is a congregation that lacks the presence of capable and anointed men of God to hold executive reins, especially a congregation that is pastored by an unmarried female pastor.

In the ordering of the church, the executive position can be assumed more easily in the joint ministry of a husband and wife when the latter, in the public exercising of her spiritual gifts, acquiesces to her husband performing the executive role of elder. Originally, this office of elder was reserved for men who were the leaders of local churches, oversaw their operation, and wielded authority over them. Because of such varying circumstances in the church, female leaders should learn to rise above any skepticisms or criticisms that confront them within or without the church community in regard to their ministries. The exercising of gifts and talents in the church may supersede the functional order of the church.

The Subordination Myth

The subordination myth had its origin in early agrarian, patriarchal cultures, such as ancient Greek, Roman, and Jewish cultures in which women were dependent economically, socially, and religiously on the superiority of men. This dependence resulted in coercion and forced submission of women to men, which weighed heavily in favor of dictatorship and against the biblical interpretation of subordination.

Historically, the depreciation of and disdain for women began in ancient Greece where there were two main thoughts regarding women. Firstly, there was the Athenian thought which supported the inferiority of women. It stipulated that women were to obey and be commanded by men and used by men for their pleasure. Secondly, there was the Stoic thought, which argued that women were a distraction to men and that men were to avoid women in order to pursue their quest for superiority.

The Athenian thought could be examined in light of the fact that women led very secluded and restricted lives. They were mainly confined to their homes, resulting in the denial of their participation in much public life. Greek women married at a young age. Their marriages were arranged, and their families paid dowries in honor of their daughters' marriages. The groom remained unknown to the bride at a wedding. Women never went out in the public alone or shared meals with any men, including their husbands. They did not join the life of the general community. A husband had the right to reject or divorce his wife without any explanation. Women were thought to obey their fathers and husbands, and Greek wives and mothers were subordinate to their husbands and sons. Wives received no formal education. They learned to cook and spin garments, and to be modest and quiet. In fact, Greek poets frequently used the word *despot* to stress and express the institutionalized belief that man was the woman's lord. A woman was expected to obey her husband and was considered mischievous if she attempted to command or rule her husband.[10]

The Stoics regarded women as a distraction to men in men's pursuit of wisdom. They supported asceticism and celibacy and believed that a celibate life led to holiness. As a result, men and women were to forsake sexual intimacy and marriage so that men could achieve spiritual development and holiness. The Stoic philosophy later infiltrated Christian thought.

The issue of control of man over woman was entrenched in ancient Roman culture where, under the patriarchal institution and law known as *patria potestas* and *manus*, a male could exercise full control over any female. A woman was required to be under male guardianship, and a wife was obligated to worship her husband's gods. She was not permitted to give orders to her husband's slaves. In the first century AD, Seneca noted that "man is born to rule and woman to obey."[11] The presence of such control compromised the positional status of women in society and, in the worst case scenario, reduced them to chattel.

In the Jewish culture, the scriptures reveal as far back as the days of Moses that a man had veto power over his wife's vow (Numbers 30:12), rendering her decision making without her husband's approval worthless. A similar trend pervaded the rabbinical era (400 BC to AD 400) when a woman was expected to submit to the directions and authority of a man, hence a woman's obligation to wash her husband's face, hands, and feet (Kathuboth 59b, 61a).[12]

The subordination of women by the Greek, Roman, and Hebrew

cultures was perpetuated by the early church fathers. For example, Clement of Alexandria believed that a man's beard was a symbol of superiority over a woman (The Instructor 3:3), and Bishop Epiphanus of Salamis (AD 315–403) felt that the ignorance of woman was proof of her subordinate status. He contended that Eve was seduced by the devil because of ignorance and that Adam could not be tempted by the devil because of his superiority.[13] In reality, however, Adam was just as guilty as Eve since he was present to witness her encounter with the devil and joined her in partaking of the fruit of the tree of the knowledge of good and evil.

In the Judeo-Christian era, theologians focused on Genesis 3:16 to justify the subordination of woman. The word *teshuqa* contained in the Hebrew text appeared in modern Bible translation to mean "desire." Thus, Genesis 3:16 partly reads, "And your desire shall be to your husband, and he shall rule over you." The Babylonian Talmud of the fifth century AD translated *teshuqa* to mean "lust." A combination of these two translations portrays women as subordinate and evil. Theologians in the Judeo-Christian era relied on these translations to promulgate their belief about the subordination of women.

The Greek Septuagint of approximately 285 BC, the oldest translations of the Old Testament, translated *teshuqa* as "turning."[14] The Cloverdale version of 1535 and the Cranmer Bible, two early English Bibles translated *teshuqa* in Solomon 7:10 as "turning." Schmidt noted that unlike *turning*, the two meanings *lust* and *desire* portrayed women in a negative way as they spoke of the need of woman sexually or otherwise to be with man and not vice versa.[15]

The substitution of the word *shall* in many English translations for the Hebrew wording of *will*, the futuristic form in "and he will rule over you" (Genesis 3:16), denoted a choice of woman based upon the condition of Eve turning away from God to Adam. Whereas *shall* is the volitional form that depicted woman as inferior and submissive to man. The alteration of this translation portrayed the inferiority and submissiveness of woman as God's command to woman.[16]

Passages of scripture in the New Testament are also used to support the subordination of women such as 1 Corinthians 11:3, Ephesians 5:22–24, and 1 Peter 3:1. These passages were written in the apostolic era of the church when women attained spiritual equality in the church. Schmidt felt that subordination in these passages of scripture might have referred to subordination in some regions only and that because of the cultural milieu of the day, freeing the church fully of the Greco-Roman culture could not be realized instantly. Likewise, the church could not radically depart from all ancient patriarchal customs since doing so could have resulted in additional persecution of the church.[17] Although Christianity is not regional, its practice may vary regionally, culturally, and denominationally.

First Corinthians 11:3 states, "But I would have you know, that the head of every man is Christ; and the head of the woman is the man; and the head of Christ is God." Ephesians 5:22–24 instructs women to "submit yourselves unto your own husbands, as unto the Lord. For the husband is the head of the wife, even as Christ is the head of the church: and he is the savior of the body. Therefore as the church is subject unto Christ, so let the wives be to their own husbands in everything." First Peter 3:1 states, "Likewise ye wives, be in subjection to your own husbands," referring to wives with nonbelieving husbands.

The issue of "headship" in these passages will be discussed in another chapter. Ephesians 5:22–24 and 1 Peter 3:1 establish a pattern within the marital relationship with respect to headship and submission. Paul used the Greek word *hupotasso* to suggest voluntary submission, based on a commitment to proper order. It honors the unique value of the wife. It stresses both value and order, as well as equality and subordination.[18] *Submit* implies a voluntary putting of oneself under another[19] and denotes no intrinsic superiority of either man or woman, but equality in the husband-wife relationship, further emphasized in 1 Peter 3:1–7. The godly submission of a wife to her husband is scriptural but does not imply or justify subordination in any shape or form whatsoever.

Greame believed that, although marriage is used as an analogy of the church in scripture, it does not necessarily mean that what applies to a marriage is relevant for the church. He pointed out that, outside the home setting, the pattern of headship and submission may not apply to the church where there are unmarried people and "other married" people.[20] Schmidt noted that theologians use these passages of scripture to permanently keep women silent and subordinate in the church setting even though they were originally used in the context of family life in the Greco-Roman era.[21] They may not necessarily be applicable in contemporary times.

Arguments for and against the Subordination of Women

The order of creation theory in Genesis 1 and 2 has been put forward to support the subordination of woman to man. There are two accounts of creation. In Genesis 1, both male and female were created in the image of God. In Genesis 2, the scriptures focus on the relationship between man and woman. In the creation accounts, the word *Adam* was used as a title for the human species. God created male and female human beings.

Complementarians regard Adam as the source, head, and representative of all humanity, which has paved the way for inequality between the sexes. Although they agree that man and woman are equal in being (Genesis 1:27), they believe that man was created first to exercise headship and that woman is functionally subordinate to man and was created after him to help him (Genesis 2:21–23, 1 Corinthians 11:8–9). A woman's function is dependent on her husband. She was created after man to follow his lead.[22]

Egalitarians argue that in its prefallen state, humanity was created by God as both man and woman in which the true essence of humanity can be found[23] and is defined. Both male and female were created in the divine image of God (Genesis 1:27) and together were to be the image of God. For this reason, Olsen pointed out that man and woman existed "in mutual belongingness and correlation with each other" and that "the image of the divine, human relatedness was designed to be one of unity and equality within the framework of complementarity." Therefore, woman was taken from man because God intended them to be complementary and compatible. Olsen further stated that when God created male and female, he did so with a major purpose in mind. The purpose for the two sexes was to reproduce. God blessed man and woman and commanded them to be fruitful and multiply and fill the earth and subdue it. Adam and Eve were to coexist in mutual dependence, with man needing woman and woman needing man. God created woman from the rib of man to exist in harmonious and equal partnership with man.[24] Man and woman were to become one flesh, enveloping each other in totality. Woman was to be man's helper (Genesis 2:18), which did not signify inferiority or a lower status, but rather equality and complementary functions as the divine helper, the Holy Spirit, performs within the Godhead. Man and woman were created of equal values to perform complementary service in love.[25]

God created two persons out of one being by making Eve, the female, out of the same substance as Adam, the male. Adam referred to Eve as "bone of my bones and flesh of my flesh" (Genesis 2:23). The difference between male and female is solely functional. The word *helper* did not signify that the female was of a lower standing than the male. Woman was created as man's helper because without her, man demonstrated a degree of helplessness. God recognized that it was not good for man to be alone and created woman to be his companion. As a result, a wife is not only a mate but a partner with her husband in their mutual quest for earthly and heavenly goals also, with each performing separate roles. A subordinate wife deserves love and kindness from her husband.[26] Since love is the basis of the relationship between a husband and wife, the husband should not misuse his God-given authority over his wife. Likewise, a wife should not exercise authority that is not God-given over her husband.

Before the fall, there was absolute equality and the absence of any form of hierarchy between man and woman. There was no evidence of the male having dominion over the female or the female having dominion over the male. Together, male and female were to have dominion over all of God's creation. There was also the absence of any shape or form of superiority of male over female. On the whole, although men may differ from women in terms of physical strength or in terms of the fact that women are more in tune with their emotions and can more readily express their emotions than men or in terms of men thinking analytically (with their heads) rather than emotionally (with their hearts), such differences do not imply that men are superior to women. Therefore, to deduce that man is superior to woman because he was created first is faulty, considering the fact that even though in the order of creation, mankind was the last to be created, he was the masterpiece of God's creation. Man and woman originated from one flesh with nothing to suggest that woman was physically weaker or inferior to man. They were both to have dominion over the earth, to replenish and subdue it (Genesis 1:28), and to unite as one flesh in marriage. God did not intend men to be superior to women. Any form of superiority of men over women was not ordained by God but was established by man through coercion and the results of sin. Since both man and woman were given dominion over the earth, no restrictions were placed on woman.

The Fall and Its Consequences

Due to man's disobedience, the harmony of nature became disrupted and disordered after the fall, severely impacting man-and-woman relationship, as well as man's relationship with God. Although Eve was the first to have sinned by eating the forbidden fruit, the ultimate responsibility for committing this offense lay with Adam to whom God had given the commandment not to partake of the forbidden tree (Genesis 2:17). He was given this commandment even before Eve was formed. Adam was much more familiar with God's creation and His command about the forbidden tree than Eve. Therefore, it was Adam who relayed God's command to Eve, thus causing any experience or knowledge she received about God's command to be vicarious. The devil did not choose to tempt Eve because she was the weaker vessel or inferior to Adam. Obviously, Eve was the more gullible in terms of her knowledge base, which made her an easier target for the onslaught of the devil. Through one man (Adam), sin entered into the world (Romans 5:12). Sin was passed down through the seed of man.

God called out to Adam in the Garden of Eden and questioned him as to whether he had eaten of the forbidden tree (Genesis 3:9, 11), which suggests that Adam and not Eve held final accountability to God for sinning since God had given the command directly to him. It further suggests that there was a more intimate relationship between Adam and God before the fall than between Eve and God. Adam attempted to pass the buck by blaming Eve for his act of disobedience. However, God had forbidden him to eat of the fruit of the tree of the knowledge of good and evil. He was present when his wife partook of the fruit and did not question her or intervene in her behalf when the devil approached her. He failed to exercise the ultimate responsibility placed upon him by God by allowing his wife to lead him into sinning. He also joined her in partaking of the fruit. In fact, he assumed a nonchalant, low-key position. He failed to assume the responsibility that God had placed on him regarding the forbidden tree and to exercise the authority that God had given to him above every creature. Notwithstanding, the last Adam, Jesus Christ, subsequently came down to earth as a spotless, sacrificial lamb to redeem mankind back to God.

Satan's temptation of Eve stresses the significance that Eve had dominion just as Adam and that her fall would be just as significant as Adam's in terms of its effect on God's creation over which they had dominion. This creation was to suffer when both Adam and Eve sinned as a result of pride and the quest for power.[27] The example set by Adam was a poor demonstration of how a godly husband should behave and a poor example for godly husbands to follow. Both Adam and Eve were equally guilty and suffered the consequences of their disobedience. They were both punished and were doomed to spiritual and physical death. Woman was to conceive and bring forth children in pain and sorrow, a sorrow that was not merely physical but was to envelop her entire life. Man was to toil for his living. His authority over woman was established. The relationship between man and woman became distorted, and they could no longer live together in harmony. Man was now to rule over woman, which implied the subordination of woman.

Inferiority Myth

In human cultures throughout history, woman has been regarded as biologically, intellectually, socially, and spiritually inferior to man. This notion has led many societies to devalue women in varying degrees and to determine their roles, functions, and positions in those societies. It has also helped to shape the views of some theologians.

The philosophers of ancient Greece were the originators of the inferiority myth and profoundly influenced the Western world's conviction that women are inferior to men. Socrates, a Greek philosopher, openly expressed his disdain for women and commented that a society built on common wife-and-children relationships would be better. He believed that a man should not be tied down to one woman.

Other Greek philosophers such as Plato and Aristotle argued that a woman is biologically inferior to a man. Aristotle described woman as a deformed male (*Generation of Animals* 2. 737a: 27). He believed that a male bee commanded a swarm of bees and that in fact, a male bee was more capable of commanding as a man in terms of humans. Aristotle was regrettably oblivious to the fact that the queen bee stands out as the most significant bee of all, which in reality commands a swarm of bees. Aristotle argued that a husband is to his wife as a soul is to a body. As the seat of wisdom and intelligence, the soul controls the actions of the arms and legs. The wife is considered a nonentity without her husband.

Plato used reincarnation to prove his theory of the inferiority of woman by saying that men who spent their lives doing wrong things and acting cowardly were reincarnated as women (Timaeus 91a).

The Greek orator, Demosthenes, gave three analyses for the roles of women in Athens. These were courtesans, prostitutes, and wives. Courtesans were wealthy prostitutes from the upper class who were used for men's pleasure. Prostitutes were young female slaves who were identified for daily use. Wives were considered as the ones to raise legitimate children and to be faithful stewards in their households.

Biological Inferiority

Like Hippocrates, the famous Greek physician, the Romans used the fetal development to support the inferiority of women. They propounded that the fetal development of a female was slower than that of a male. The assumption that was made from the common belief about the slower development of a female fetus was that woman lacked the physical perfection of a man and was therefore inferior.

Women were expected to marry at a young age, which resulted in a high female mortality rate during their pregnancy and childbirth, giving rise to the notion that women were weaker than men. An identified cause of this high mortality rate among women was that girls were given poorer nourishment than boys although more male fetuses were miscarried. Until the early centuries, men outlived women by about four to seven years. Women's life expectancy rose in the Middle Ages with the advent of an urban economy and continues to be on the rise. Today, a large percentage of women outlive their spouses even though more women are now in the labor force and, in some cases, are the primary breadwinners of their families.

Jewish thought was profoundly influenced and transformed by the Athenian and Stoic philosophies. For example, a Jewish scholar named Philo attempted to interpret Old Testament scriptures through the teachings of Greek philosophers such as Aristotle and Plato. Both Philo and Josephus, a Jewish historian, viewed women with disdain.

Intellectual Inferiority

Intellectually, women were also considered inferior in the agrarian cultures of the Greek and Roman societies. This belief was perpetuated by Gentile converts who were influenced by Greek philosophies regarding women, by the church fathers in the early church, as well as by free thinkers, physicians, and educators as late as in the twentieth century.

Some theologians in the Christian faith that used Greek philosophy for interpreting the scriptures were Tertullian, Saint Augustine, Clement of Alexandria, Martin Luther, and Thomas Aquinas. For example, Thomas Aquinas said that women were not perfect enough in wisdom.[28] Martin Luther felt that "Adam was wiser than Eve in the fall"[29] and that "a man is nobler than a woman."[30] A common belief was that man possessed intelligence because they had broad shoulders and narrow hips. By no means can intellect be measured by broad shoulders and narrow hips.

Dr. William H. Walling was one of the many physicians in the twentieth century who supported the intellectual inferiority of women. He argued that too much mental stimulation was harmful for pubescent girls.[31] Despite the various opinions expressed for centuries by several proponents of female inferiority, it has not yet been proven that men are indeed intellectually superior to women. Some women are just as capable as some men of excelling in various fields and professions, including in the ministry.

Social Inferiority

It is believed that the social inferiority theory about women emerged after 2400 BC when women were forbidden to practice polyandry, own or control much property, receive equal rank or economic rewards with men, or perform spiritual exercises equal to men.[32] As the Sumerian culture emerged, the status of women declined. The status of women in other cultures such as the Hebrew, Greek, and Roman cultures was also adversely affected. In the Hebrew culture, wives were expected to address their husbands by their names and titles as how slaves addressed their masters. The birth of a son was far more valuable than that of a daughter. In Greece, a woman could not leave her house unless an adult accompanied her. Wives had no formal education and were barred from listening in public to male philosophers and from the all-male council known as Areopagus where decisions were made. Only mistresses known as hetaerae who were well educated could participate in these activities. In the Roman culture, women were bound by their fathers' names as long as they were under their control. They could not participate in their husbands' occupations and knew little about their affairs. They could not plead in court and had limited inheritance. Husbands could divorce their wives for appearing in public unveiled.[33]

Spiritual Inferiority

Some ancient cultures also taught that a woman was spiritually inferior to a man. In the Hebrew society, only sons were to be taught religious teachings by their fathers as commanded in the fourth, sixth, and eleventh chapters of Deuteronomy. It was considered lewdness for girls to be taught the law. The rite of circumcision was extended only to boys, thus making them qualified to receive the privileges and blessings of God. Women could not participate in public worship in the synagogues. They had to be veiled and silent while the men chanted or sang.

Several theologians in early Christendom supported the belief that women were not created in the image of God like men or that the image of God in them was inferior to that in men. For example, Isidore, a sixth-century archbishop of Spain contended that woman was in the image of man for whom she was made and that man was in the image of God (Sententiæ 10, 4–6). In the thirteenth century, Thomas Aquinas taught that God's image in man differed from that in woman because man was the beginning and end of woman (Summa Theologiae 1a, 93:5).[34] A twentieth-century German Lutheran theologian, Emil Brunner, propagated that the mental and spiritual natures of woman were created different from those of man.[35] However, according to Genesis 1:26–27, God created the human species, both man and woman, in His image.

Many scholars and theologians regarded celibacy as the route to personal holiness. Women were viewed as objects of sexuality, which was considered a snare of the devil to distract men from attaining holiness, and therefore, men were to avoid women at any cost.

Early Christian Attitudes toward Women

The philosophical and cultural biases against women became entrenched in cultures of the known world as far back as the fourth century BC when Alexander the Great was on a mission to inculcate the Greek way of life into other cultures. He was considered to be one of the most brilliant military leaders in those days, and he had conquered the then-known world in the third century BC. He was trained by Aristotle and was an ardent proponent of Greek culture. He attempted to spread the Greek culture to all the lands that he conquered. This process was known as Hellenization, a process which successors of Alexander were committed to perpetuating after Alexander's death at age thirty-three.

For centuries, women were devalued and depreciated. Those biases were present in the Jewish society when Jesus Christ and Paul appeared upon the scene. Women were regarded as morally weak and easily led astray as in the account of Adam and Eve in the fall. A Rabbi might not speak to his daughter or sister in public, and a Jewish male would thank God every morning in a recital for not being a Gentile, woman, or boor. Some Pharisees were called the bruised or bleeding ones because they would walk into walls and houses as a result of closing their eyes whenever they saw women on the streets. Women could not be taught the Torah and were mainly uneducated.[36] They were regarded as chattel and as possessions of their husbands if they were married or of their fathers if they were unmarried (Deuteronomy 5:21).

However, not all nations and Greeks agreed with the Athenian and Stoic views of women. For example, the women of Sparta exercised tremendous freedom and political responsibilities. At one time, they owned about two-thirds of the land. Unlike Athens, Sparta did not leave any philosophical legacy to the world.

Egyptian women enjoyed a great amount of freedom from living in an egalitarian society. They held equal status with men, obtained equal legal rights as men, and participated in politics. In marriage, they acquired equal rights and privileges as their husbands. Egyptian women could sit on local tribunals, engage in real estate transactions, acquire and bequeath property, and obtain loans on their property. They could adopt children and buy, sell, or free slaves. They could witness legal documents and represent themselves on legal matters.

At the dawn of the Christian era, Roman women had begun to enjoy freedom as well on a relatively large scale. As citizens of Rome by birth or marriage, they acquired the right to own and dispose a property and were in control of their persons. They were able to freely appear in public and to attend religious services, public games, and the theater. They were involved in every sphere of life in Rome, influenced the administration of the country, and studied philosophy. Roman matrons were free to arrange their marriages, to marry of their own free will, and to live with their husbands as their moral and intellectual equals. Both parties could initiate divorce proceedings for no specific reasons. As a result, divorce became rampant, and family life suffered in Rome. This rise in women's status caused women in the early church to play a significant role in the spread of Christianity.

In the Greco-Roman world, there was a paucity of religious options that could be exercised by women although there were two basic forms of religion, namely, native cults and oriental cults. Judaism and Christianity were among the religious options.

There were some very prestigious women who participated in religion. These were six public priestesses, known as the vestal virgins. They tended the fire in the Temple of Vesta in the Roman Forum and were expected to remain chaste throughout their thirty years' service but could get married subsequently. They were among the most liberated of Roman women and were not legally bound to husbands or fathers. They held powerful positions in public and legal rights like men.

Apart from their participation in state religious festivals, women could participate in many private religious organizations in which they could perform leadership roles.[37] In fact, in both Judaism and Christianity, women could perform prestigious roles even though the extent to which they wielded power and authority might never be known because of the preponderance of cultural bias in the information handed down to posterity. Thurston cited Bernadette Brooten in her book *Women Leaders in the Ancient Synagogue* as saying that women were prominent as financial supporters, heads, and elders of synagogues.[38]

Jesus Christ and Women

When Jesus Christ appeared on the scene, His revolutionary actions ran counter to the social and religious norms of His day and defied the entrenched cultural practices and taboos through women who experienced freedom, which Jesus Christ brought and encouraged. He taught women, came in contact with a menstruating woman, spoke to women in public, affirmed their spiritual gifts, welcomed them as disciples, and accepted their support. "By thus honoring them, He put woman on an equality with man, demanding the same standard from both sexes and offering the same way of salvation" (Beeching 1982:1259).[39] Women became persons of worth and objects of His grace and proceeded to play a prominent role in the spread of Christianity.

Many women took readily to Christianity that opposed the Greco-Roman culture, which required them to honor and worship the gods of their husbands. They were liberated from the law that existed for centuries, to follow the religious beliefs of their choice, and to which they were attracted. Jesus Christ treated them with dignity and elevated them to new heights above the ancient laws and taboos that kept them in subordination and discriminated against them for centuries.

Several examples could be drawn from the scriptures where Jesus Christ performed liberating acts toward women. He reestablished oneness and equality between man and woman in the order of creation and emphasized the sanctity of marriage. The Mosaic law permitted a man to divorce his wife at will by issuing her a certificate of divorce, but the wife was disallowed from doing likewise (Leviticus 21:7, 14). In addressing the issue of divorce from a question he was asked by the Pharisees, Jesus Christ explained that divorce took place under the Mosaic law because of the hardness of people's hearts. He emphasized the permanence of marriage by stating that God created male and female, that the two shall become one flesh, and that "what therefore God has joined together, let no man put asunder" (Mark 10:2–9).

Women were visible as followers of Jesus Christ. They listened to His teachings alongside men (Luke 8:1–3, 11:27, 23:27–28; Mark 15:40–41). In reality, women were not included in the inner circle around Jesus Christ based on the cultural context of that day. However, France noted, according to Luke 8:1–3, that the inner circle was not very sharply distinct from the wider group, which included women.[40] Some of these women financially supported Jesus Christ's ministry, for example, Mary Magdalene, Joanna the wife of Chuza, and Suzanna (Luke 8:1–3). Jesus Christ treated His women followers with the same respect and dignity as He treated His male disciples.[41] This was a radical departure from the religious segregation that occurred in ancient worship in the temples and synagogues where women sat in a court and gallery apart from men.[42] He destroyed the artificial man-made, cultural, and social barriers by openly teaching women theology.

In ancient times, women were forbidden to study the Torah. The story of Mary and Martha clearly exemplifies Jesus Christ's desire for women to hear the Word of God (Luke 11:38–42). Martha was content to perform the traditional role of preparing a meal for Jesus Christ while her sister, Mary, exercised her newly found liberty to being taught the Word of God. Martha expressed concern about being left alone to serve Jesus Christ who readily sanctioned Mary's liberated act, contrary to the religious norms that forbade women to study the Word of God as stipulated in Hebraic rabbinic teachings. Martha in this story was the same Martha to whom Jesus Christ revealed the axiom of the Christian faith as recorded in John 11:25–26, which states, "I am the resurrection and the life: he who believes in me, though he were dead yet shall he live: and whoever lives and believes in me shall never die."

Jesus Christ performed other liberating acts. He called a woman who had an infirmity for eighteen years into the synagogue (Luke 13:11–13) where women were forbidden to interact with worshipping men, spoke to her, and permitted her to speak as she began to praise God in violation of the oral laws of the Rabbis, which said, "The voice of a woman (in public) is shameful" (Berakhoth 24a).[43] His encounter with the Samaritan woman transcended religious and ethnic barriers. The Samaritans were forbidden to worship in Jerusalem, and the Jews regarded them as inferior and had no dealings with them. In talking with a Samaritan woman in public, Jesus Christ violated the rabbinic religious doctrines that forbade Him to speak with a woman in public, moreover with a Samaritan woman.[44] After Jesus Christ taught her theology (John 4:24) by imparting to her that God is a Spirit and that they who worship Him must worship Him in spirit and in truth, the Samaritan woman became the first female evangelist in the history of Christianity. We learn that as a result of her testimony, many Samaritans believed in Jesus Christ (John 4:39).

Jesus Christ interacted with two unclean women in public. One of them was a prostitute who washed His feet with her tears, wiped them with her hair, kissed them, and anointed them with expensive ointment in the house of a Pharisee named Simon. The unorthodox action of Jesus Christ drew criticism from Simon, the host. After affirming her human worth and spiritual gift, Jesus Christ spoke directly to her and said, "Thy sins are forgiven" (Luke 7:37–48). The second woman had been menstruating for twelve long years and pressed forward in a crowd to touch the helm of Jesus's garment. According to Leviticus 15:19, which states that "whoever touches her shall be unclean until the evening," that woman was unclean. Now according to this law, Jesus Christ was rendered unclean and needed to engage in a purification ritual to cleanse Himself. Not only did He forgo this ritual, but He spoke directly to the woman and said, "Daughter, thy faith hath made thee whole, go in peace and be whole of thy plague" (Mark 5:34).

At the crucifixion of Jesus Christ, His women followers showed resilience, commitment, and faithfulness after the male disciples had forsaken Jesus Christ. They lingered at the cross, saw His burial, and looked after its ritual needs. It is not surprising then that they were the first to learn of His resurrection. All four of the Gospels support the stark reality of Jesus Christ revealing His messiahship and His resurrection from the dead to women first (Matthew 28:1–8; Mark 16:1–8; Luke 24:1–12; John 20:1–17). Although the male disciples initially regarded the women's report of the resurrection of Jesus Christ as senseless babble (Luke 24:11),[45] the women's testimony eventually prevailed as recorded in Luke 24:22–24 through the two disciples whom Jesus encountered en route to Emmaus.[46]

Paul and Women

In His treatment of women, Jesus Christ left a legacy for Paul to follow in his view of and interaction with women. Paul visualized equality among people in the kingdom of God, irrespective of their racial or ethnic background, gender, or financial status. He attempted to deviate from the Hellenized mind-set to the Christian way of thinking that required a transformation of the minds and thoughts of a people who were conditioned to cultural, social, and religious biases pertaining to women. His goal was to foster a new standard of equality for male and female in the Christian community. In providing insight into the status of women in early Christianity, Paul used the baptismal formula as the primary rite of initiation into equal membership in the community of Christ. He stated in Galatians 3:27, "For as many of you as have been baptized into Christ have put on Christ." Water baptism marks the beginning of the unity of all believers in Christ regardless of their race, class, or gender (Romans 10:12; 1 Corinthians 12:8; Colossians 3:11). They are entitled to the same benefits that result from their union with Christ and have become the children of God, offspring of Abraham, and heirs of the promise (Galatians 3:26, 29).[47] Paul stressed the importance of "oneness in Christ." He made it clear that "There is neither Jew nor Greek, there is neither bond nor free, there is neither male nor female, for you are all one in Christ Jesus" (Galatians 3:28). His declaration that there is no distinction in Christ based on sex, race, or social standing was an attempt to elevate the status of women, especially in the Middle East.

Before Paul appeared upon the scene, the uncircumcised Gentiles were unequal to the devout Jews who stood out from the Gentiles by their observation of the Sabbath and other festivals such as Passover and Hanukkah by dietary restrictions and by circumcision. In addition, the Pharisees observed the rules of cleanliness and uncleanliness and of tithing. Paul was commissioned to reach the Gentiles with the Gospel of Christ and recognized the inequality of the Gentiles to the Jews before God. This notion was encouraged among the early Christians.[48]

In addressing the issue of equality and oneness in Christ, Grenz and Kjesbo examined complementarian and egalitarian views on this matter. They noted that Complementarians regard equality (and oneness) in Christ as relating only to the position of the redeemed. Complementarians do not subscribe to the social equality between male and female. Grenz and Kjesbo cited Robert Saucy as saying, "The thrust of these statements is the truth that all are equally sons of God, all are equally clothed with Christ, all are equally heirs of the promise."⁴⁹ They stated that Egalitarians see Galatians 3:28 as the foundation for a new social order in the church. As the "Magna Carta of Humanity," this passage of scripture emancipated women in their role as believers and subscribed to both equality of stereological position and function before God.⁵⁰ Grenz and Kjesbo quoted Klyne Snodgrass who described Galatians 3:28 as "the most socially explosive text in the Bible" and who said, "There is nothing in the Christian faith that is merely coram Deo [before God]. All of our faith engages all of our lives."⁵¹

Egalitarians believe that it was Paul's intention for the church community to practice the unity and faith it experienced in Christ. This belief applied not only to Jews and Gentiles, bond and free, but also to male and female relations. Grenz and Kjesbo quoted Bruce in his commentary on the epistle to the Galatians as saying, "No more restriction is implied in Paul's equalizing of the status of Jews and Gentiles, or of slave and free person. If, in ordinary life, existence in Christ is manifested openly in church fellowship, then, if a Gentile may exercise spiritual leadership in church as freely as a Jew, or a slave as freely as a citizen, why not a woman as freely as a man?"⁵²

Ben Witherington interpreted Paul's declaration in Galatians 3:28 as a female not having to be linked to a male to have a place in the church community, as the roles of women not being limited to wife or mother, and as the door to the ministry being opened to women, including the ministry of single women.⁵³ In 1 Corinthians 7:34–35, Paul strengthened the position of single persons in the church community, thus paving the way for women to remain single by choice to concentrate on the ministry and to assume roles in the Christian community besides mother and wife.

Paul's hope to develop equality between the sexes went against the grain of embedded attitudes that were established by the Stoics and by the Greek and Jewish laws. Aristotle's devaluation of women contradicted Paul's ideas about women. Aristotle saw a female as a deformed male⁵⁴ whereas Paul declared that male and female are one in Christ (Galatians 3:28). Aristotle contended that women were inferior to men in their ability to reason.⁵⁵ In 1 Timothy 2:11, Paul supported women learning, even though in silence. Greek and Jewish laws stated that the authority over a woman belonged first to her father and then, after marriage, to her husband. Paul said that a woman shall have authority on her own head (1 Corinthians 11:10).

Patriarchy in the Church

Paul was a champion for oneness, equality, and functional complementarity. However, this oneness and equality did not mean sameness but spoke of interdependence where a man remained male and a woman remained female.[56] Paul's ideas gained momentum until the middle of the fourth century AD that even Tertullian, who expressed ambivalence about women in his writings, made the following comment based on his observation of men and women in the church. They "perform their fasts, mutually teaching, mutually exhorting, mutually sustaining. Equally are they both found in the church of God; equally in straits, in persecution, in refreshments. Neither hides from the other; neither shuns the other; neither is troublesome to the other."[57] Female martyrs such as the slave girl Blandina of Lyons (177), the lady Perpetua and her slave Felicity in Carthage (202) are recorded in the annals of history, a testimony that women paid their dues in like manner as men.

By the middle of the fourth century, Paul's idea of equality had begun to crumble when the church began to accept favors from the state. Emperor Constantine fostered this close alliance between the church and the state and expected the priests to accompany the troops to battle to boost their military morale. Women were excluded from the organization of the church as they could not serve in this capacity. It was also argued that too many women were involved in the mystery cults that were practiced in Rome, which also affected their ability to accompany the troops to battle.

In response to their exclusion from the organization of the church, women began to express an interest in education and in the establishment of schools. For example, one of Constantine's daughters founded the first women's cloister, and his mother, Helena, built a hospice for pilgrims. A woman named Fabiola established the first hospital in Rome. By the fourth century, woman could no longer teach in the church, and their actual work in the church could not be clearly determined. They failed to challenge the subordinate role and position they were made to adapt in the structure of the church. They might have been too busy spreading the Gospel, which could have been responsible for their failure to respond to the changes that occurred within the structure of the church.[58]

Gradually, a mixture of Christian theology and Greek philosophy emerged in the church, resulting in many pagan assumptions. One assumption that was accepted by church leaders in the fourth century was that sexual intimacy and marriage were detrimental to one's spirituality. The writings of the church father like Augustine had a tremendous impact on the church while the teachings of Aristotle were accepted as almost infallible. The ideas of Augustine and Aristotle caused church leaders to have sexual biases toward women and to interpret Paul's writings in like manner.[59] God's intent and purpose for instituting marriage in the Garden of Eden was for humans to procreate. Sexual intimacy and marriage are not meant to be detrimental to anyone's spirituality. The ideas of Aristotle and Augustine contradict God's command to Adam and Eve to be fruitful and multiply.

Paul's teachings regarding male and female equality and oneness in Christ were challenged by such church fathers as Augustine, Thomas Aquinas, Martin Luther, and John Calvin. Augustine emphasized the subordination of woman to man as the order of nature. He believed that woman reflected the nature of God only in her oneness with her husband. She is not the image of God when referred to as her husband's "helpmeet."[60] Martin Luther saw woman as a sex object for the purpose of procreation and interpreted the curse of Genesis 3:16 as the rule remaining with the husband and the wife's compulsion to obey her husband as commanded by God.[61] In his teachings on women, Calvin propounded that the married woman should serve, honor, and reverence her husband, while the single woman should be sober and modest and acknowledge man as her superior and ruler.[62] Aquinas did not subscribe to the equality of man and woman before or after the fall.[63] Like Aristotle, he regarded women as "defective and misbegotten." He interpreted Galatians 3:28, "There is neither male nor female, for you are all one in Christ Jesus," as the social union of man and woman.[64] He believed that woman was subjected to man from the beginning of time and that there were varying degrees in which man and woman were created in the image of God. Although both male and female have the ability to understand and love God, only the male "actually and habitually knows and loves God."[65]

This depreciation of womanhood was contrary to the very intent and purpose for which Paul wrote Galatians 3:28. He intended it to be a declaration of sexual equality among Christians. Buhrig noted that the church fathers, like the writers of the New Testament and beyond, had been males who propagated their biased views about women. These views permeated Christian theology and lent credence to the notion of male domination that is firmly established in the structure of the church.

Paul also intended Galatians 3:28 to demonstrate the spiritual equality of male and female in the church. Hamilton and Hamilton aptly pointed out Paul's full awareness that this spiritual unity of male and female in Christ resulted in the abolition of all differences among human beings, such as differences of sex. However, they concluded that Paul discouraged women from actually participating in the services of the local congregation. They acknowledged that women played a prominent part in New Testament history and that they were associated with the Apostles and that they were at the center of the church movement. It was because of the cultural milieu of Paul's day, which supported female subordination and male domination, that Paul discouraged women from actively participating in the services of the local congregation. It is believed that some Greek philosophers and church fathers scrutinized Paul's views about women because they ran counter to the cultural milieu of those times. Because of the social structures that existed then, it was unthinkable for women to be leaders in the new movement. The twelve Apostles chosen by Jesus Christ were men, and men fully directed the early church, which negates the fact that Paul was supportive of women leaders, for example, in house churches. The spiritual equality of men and women was downplayed in history even though both male and female saints and martyrs were honored by Christians during the years of persecution under the Roman government, and women continued to make great names for themselves down the ages.[66]

Male domination in the church rose to prominence with the church fathers under whom leadership became all male after power, domination, and subordination were abolished in the community created by Jesus Christ. In this community, the barriers of segregation were lifted, thus creating a unique oneness in the body of Christ. If the subordination of women were to be reinforced in the church, then this subordination might have had to be viewed in a positive way. Therefore, a woman's willingness to be subordinate to a man could be regarded as a show of strength rather than one of weakness and servility.[67]

Participants of the African Regional Consultation held at the Center for Church and Society in Ibadan, Nigeria, in September 1980 discussed the reinforcement of the sexual and spiritual equality of male and female in Christ. The representatives consisted of an equal number of men and women who examined Genesis 2. They concluded that man was created from mud, and woman from man, which makes woman in no way inferior to man. They agreed that "bone of my bones and flesh of my flesh" (Genesis 2:23) indicated that man and woman became one flesh and equals. They believed that the original meaning of "helper" did not signify subordination or an inferior position. They drew attention to the fact that in the scriptures, God is referred to as "our helper" and that some people who are helpers or in helping positions, such as doctors and teachers, may be regarded as other people's equals or superiors. As our helper, God is supreme, omnipotent, omnipresent, omniscient, and transcendent.[68]

---

1. Louise Rushmore, "The Role of Women in the Church." [Online] Available http://www.hope_of_israel.org/women.htm (5/14/2004), 1.
2. "Role of Women in the Church 1 Corinthians 11:1–16." [Online]. Available http://www.angelfire.com/nt/theology/1cr11-01.html (5/14/2004), 3–4.
3. Stanley J. Grenz with Denise Muir Kjesbo, *Women in the Church: A Biblical Theology of Women in Ministry* (Downers Grove, Illinois: InterVarsity Press, 1995), 151, cited from Thomas R. Schreiner, "Head Coverings, Prophecies and the Trinity: 1 Corinthians 11:2–16," in *Recovering Biblical Manhood and Womanhood: A Response to Evangelical Feminism*, eds. John Piper and Wayne Grudem (Wheaton, Illinois: Crossway, 1991), 128.
4. Herbert Lockyer, *All the Doctrines of the Bible: A Study and Analysis of Major Bible Doctrines* (Grand Rapids, Michigan 49530: Zondervan Publishing House, 1964), 123.
5. Ibid.
6. Stanley J. Grenz with Denise Muir Kjesbo, op. cit., 152.
7. Richard R. Melick Jr., PhD, "Women Pastors: What Does the Bible Teach." [Online] Available http://www.baptist2baptist.com/b2article.asp?ID=229 (5/13/2004). 6.
8. Roy L. Barker, et al. "The Ministry of Women," *Ministry in the Seventies*, ed. Clive Porthouse (London: Falcon Books, 1970), 104.
9. Ibid.
10. Alvin John Schmidt, *Veiled and Silenced: How Culture Shaped Sexist Theology* (Macon, Georgia 31207: Mercer University Press, 1990), 85–86.
11. Ibid., 86.
12. Ibid., 86–87.
13. Ibid., 87.
14. Ibid., 87–88.
15. Ibid., 88.
16. Ibid., 88–89.
17. Ibid., 91.
18. Melick, op. cit., 4.
19. Greame's Home Page, A Theological and Biblical Exposition of the Role of Women and Their Relationship to Men within the Church, with Special Reference to Authority and Teaching. [Online] Available www.youth.co.za/papers/wommin.htm, 22/04/2001, 3, in John Piper and Wayne Grudem, eds. *Recovering Biblical Manhood and Womanhood* (Wheaton: Crossways Books 1991), 166.

20. Ibid.
21. Schmidt, op. cit., 90.
22. Bonnidell Clouse and Robert G. Clouse, eds., *Women in Ministry: Four Views* (Downers Grove, Illinois 60515: InterVarsity Press, 1989), cited from Susan Foh, "A Male Leadership View: The Head of the Woman Is the Man," 72–74.
23. Graeme, op. cit., 1, in Paul K. Jewett, *Man as Male and Female* (Grand Rapids, Michigan: William B. Eerdmans Publishing Company, 1975), 49.
24. V. Norkov Olsen, *The New Relatedness for Man & Woman in Christ: A Mirror of the Divine* (California: Loma Linda, 1993), 44–46.
25. Ibid., 50.
26. Rushmore, op. cit., 2.
27. "The Place of Women," [Online] Available http://www.pursuingthetruth.org/studies/files/placeofwomen.htm, 10–12, in *A Scriptural Perspective on the Place of Women*, © 2000 William R. Cunningham, Second Edition: February 7, 2001.
28. Schmidt, op. cit., 69–74.
29. Ibid., 74, in Martin Luther, "Lectures on 1 Timothy," *Commentaries on 1 Corinthians 7, 1 Corinthians 15, Lectures on 1 Timothy, Luther's Works*. Vol. 28, ed. Hilton C. Oswald (St. Louis: Concordia Publishing Company, 1973), 278.
30. Ibid., 74, in Martin Luther, "Commentary on 1 Corinthians 7," *Luther's Works*, 28:16.
31. Ibid., 76, in William H. Welling, *Sexology* (Philadelphia: Puritan Publishing Company, 1904), 207.
32. Ibid., 77, in Samuel Noah Kramer, *The Sumerians: Their History, Culture and Character* (Chicago University Press, 1962).
33. Ibid., 78–80.
34. Ibid., 82–84.
35. Ibid., 84, in Emil Brunner, *The Divine Imperative* (New York: MacMillan, 1937), 375.
36. Bonnie Thurston, *Women in the New Testament: Questions and Commentary* (New York: The Crossroad Publishing Company, 1998), 21–28.
37. Ibid., 18.
38. Graeme's Home Page, op. cit., 9.
39. R. T. France, *Women in the Church's Ministry: A Test Case for Biblical Interpretation* (Grand Rapids, Michigan: William B. Eerdmans Publishing Company, 1995), 78.
40. Dr. Loren L. Johns, "Women in Ministry According to the New Testament: An Exegetical and Theological Issue" [Online] Available http//www.ambs.edu/LJohns/women.htm, 22/04/2001, 5.
41. Olsen, op. cit., 88.
42. Schmidt, op. cit., 92–93.
43. Ibid., 165–167.
44. France, op. cit., 78.
45. Johns, op. cit., 4–5.
46. Grenz with Kjesbo, op. cit., 99–100.
47. Aida Besançon Spencer, *Beyond the Curse: Women Called to Ministry* (Nashville. Camden. New York: Thomas Nelson Publishers, 1985), 65–67.

48. Grenz with Kjesbo, op. cit. 100, from Robert L. Saucy, "The Negative Case against the Ordination of Women," in *Perspectives on Evangelical Theology: Papers from the Thirtieth Annual Meeting of the Evangelical Theological Society*, eds. Kenneth S. Kantzer and Stanley N. Gundry (Grand Rapids, Michigan: Baker, 1979), 281.
49. Ibid., 101, from Paul K. Jewett, *Man as Male and Female: A Study in Sexual Relationships from a Theological Point of View* (Grand Rapids, Michigan: Eerdmans, 1975), 142.
50. Ibid., cited from Klyne R. Snodgrass, "The Ordination of Women-Thirteen Years Later: Do We Really Value the Ministry of Women?" *Covenant Quarterly* 48, no.3 (August 1990): 34–35.
51. Ibid., 104, from F. F. Bruce, *Commentary on Galatians*, 188–189.
52. Ibid., 106, from Ben Witherington III, "Rite and Rights for Women-Galatians 3:28," *New Testament Studies* 27, no. 5 (1981), 600.
53. John Temple Bristow, *What Paul Really Said about Women: An Apostle's Liberating Views on Equality in Marriage, Leadership and Love* (San Francisco: Harper, 1991), 111, from Aristotle, *On the Generation of Animals*, trans. O. M. Balme (Oxford: Clarendon, 1972), 2.3.737A.
54. Ibid., from Aristotle, *Politics*, trans. Oxford University, *The Basic Works of Aristotle*, Richard McKean, editor (New York: Random House, 1941) 1.1259B.
55. Ibid.
56. Olsen, op. cit., 103.
57. Bristow, op. cit., 112, from Tertullian, *Anti-Nicene Fathers*, trans. S. Thelwall (New York: Scribner's 1885), 4.48.
58. Elsie Thomas Culver, *Women in the World of Religion* (Garden City, New York: Doubleday & Company, 1967), 73–75.
59. Ibid., 113–114.
60. Olsen, op. cit., 72.
61. Ibid., 77–78.
62. Ibid., 79–80.
63. Bristow, op. cit., 115, from Aquinas, *Summa*, Q. 92, art.1.
64. Ibid., 116, Q. 92, art. 3.
65. Ibid., 117, Q. 93, art. 4.
66. Kenneth and Alice Hamilton, *To Be a Man, To Be a Woman* (Nashville and New York: Abingdon Press, 1972), 150–151.
67. Ibid., 154.
68. John C. B. and Ellen Low Webster, eds., *The Church and Women in the Third World* (Philadelphia: The Westminster Press, 1985), 114.

Chapter Two:
Leadership—Authority, Power, and Submission

The role of leadership performed by women in ministry has resulted in varying degrees of controversy in the body of Christ. Although women have always outnumbered men in the faith community and have played a significant part in the mainstay of the church historically, they have been denied positions of leadership in many cases except under male direction, or they have been confined to leadership roles in fringe or marginalized areas of ministry. Women may not be welcome to leadership positions in some evangelical denominations although they have been very instrumental in Christian worship and life throughout the history of the church. Men have overshadowed the presence of women because of a male hierarchy that restricts leadership by women. Therefore, it is crucial to examine the three components of leadership—authority, power, and submission as they apply to women in ministry.

Jesus Christ exemplified the definition of leadership and demonstrated by word and deed that leadership embodies servanthood. In His teachings, He emphasized mutual ministry and servant leadership. Quoting Matthew 20:26–28, Jesus said, "And whosoever will be chief among you, let him be your servant: Even as the Son of man came not to be ministered unto, but to minister and to give his life a ransom for many."

The word *ministry* is derived from the Greek word *diakonia* that means *service*. However, Hageman noted that women who wish to serve in the church are confronted with two problems. Firstly, for them, ministry may be associated with a minister or a priest, and in turn, with a dominant all-male caste system. Secondly, women dislike identifying with the servant role, which signifies oppression. To hear that they are called to be servants may not be any good news for some women.[1]

Women everywhere are seeking for some clarity regarding the meaning of being a servant for Christ. Does becoming a servant for Christ bear the same connotation for men and for women? With respect to women, Parvey viewed the concept of becoming servants for Christ to mean only certain types of spiritual models and roles given in the past to women by men under male authority. This meaning evokes a stifling and crippling feeling since it prohibits female leaders from exercising their freedom in Christ, to operate in the roles and positions in which God has placed them. As a result, women are now seeking some clarity in way of a redefinition of servanthood based on the scriptures and one which encourages relationships of mutual responsibility between men and women to embrace the ever-changing needs and visions of ministry and servanthood.[2]

Leadership in the church transcends human gender. It is an embodiment of the indiscriminate call of God to serve humanity and is inextricably linked with ministry, which means service. A person who is called to the ministry is called to serve, thus emulating the example set by Jesus Christ, the humblest of servants who ever lived.

Grenz and Kjesbo noted that the central task of completing the work of the church is the giftedness of God's people, which occurs when everyone (male and female) uses his or her Spirit-endowed gifts to carry out the church's mandate (Romans 12:3–8; 1 Corinthians 12:4–31; 1 Peter 4:10–11).[3] It follows, then, that women should be allowed unhindered to exercise whatever gifts the Holy Spirit entrusts to them.

Hageman discussed some truisms about the concept of ministry. Firstly, ministry in the church is derived from the threefold functions of Christ, namely *Prophet, Priest,* and *King.* Secondly, all people of God are called to the ministry even though only some people are set apart by clerical ordination. Thirdly, there is a varied pattern of ministry, such as bishops and deacons.[4] If all of God's people are called to the ministry, which means service, and servant leadership is the primary function of the church's mandate, where then does the crux of the problem lie for women leaders in ministry? It lies within the significant and prestigious representative roles of ministry. The Eucharist or the Lord's Supper is one of the most vital representative functions.

Women leaders, especially those who are ordained, are required as their male counterparts to represent their local congregations within the wider

Christian fellowship, to represent the church to the world, and to be the representatives of Christ. Complementarians argue that only males can be representatives of Christ in celebrating the Eucharist or Lord's Supper. In the Roman Catholic Church, only male priests can act "in the person of Christ" (*in persona Christi*), a belief that gained momentum in Protestantism as well. This belief emerged from the Doctrine of Transubstantiation in which the elements of bread and wine actually become the body and blood of Jesus Christ, a Eucharist doctrine that came into existence in the Middle Ages with such proponents as Thomas Aquinas. His doctrine supports the idea of the priest assuming the role and image of Jesus Christ or the impersonation of Jesus Christ. As a result, only a man should officiate at the Communion or Lord's Supper observance because he best represents the maleness of Jesus Christ.

Complementarians put forward the argument of the ontological representation of Christ in which the ordained minister embodies the actual nature of Jesus Christ as a platform for excluding women leaders from being ordained.[5] The issue of ordination will be examined in more detail in chapter 4. Since Jesus Christ officiated as Priest when He instituted the Lord's Supper, this line of argument does not only prohibit women from ordained ministry but also denies their right as believers to be priests under God to carry out the Great Commission (Matthew 28:19–20). Bloomquist noted that even when women have been given authority in the church, they have often been denied the right to preside over the Eucharist, which she regarded as the high point of the church's life. This being so, she felt that the church will continue to represent unwholeness for women.[6]

Grenz and Kjesbo drew two conclusions regarding the representative function of ministers. Firstly, they concluded that this function is fundamentally vocal rather than actual. The person who officiates is the mouthpiece of Jesus Christ, the true host who invites people to partake of the Sacrament. Nothing, including ordination or gender, should prohibit a believer from officiating, thus supporting the Priesthood of Believers doctrine. Secondly, they concluded that limiting the Eucharist to the officiation of males demonstrates an insufficient and incorrect understanding of this event. They believed that the Eucharist doctrine might be enhanced if both male and female represented Jesus Christ at the Lord's Table.[7]

Authority

Many definitions have been put forward for leadership to highlight certain qualities and abilities. Two of these qualities are humility and creativity. Some abilities are the abilities to create community, to motivate, to manage in way of planning, organizing, and making decisions, to act as representative of a group, to envision goals and affirm values, and to revitalize a community. In the biblical context, leadership embraces servanthood, authority, and power that emanate from God. In reality, leadership empowers.

In order for biblical authority to be clearly understood, it must be viewed in the context of the Bible, which is the basis of authority. The Bible is the authoritative Word of God whose character provides an indispensable source of knowledge for the church and leads men to the faith.[8] The Holy Spirit helps in its interpretation, with Jesus Christ being the author of our faith. Jesus Christ was endowed with authority that was derived from God the Father. Langley noted that such authority was unworldly and was exercised through obedient services that could possibly culminate in death (Isaiah 53). She contended that similar authority is given to the church. Hence, Christian ministers are to emulate Jesus Christ. Since God Himself calls people to official leadership positions in the church and to servanthood, the same mode of recognition of servanthood should be used for both men and women. This call comes with no known distinction based on gender, race, or any other criteria. Authority given by God is not meant for a person to lord it over others, but rather, it is meant for service to God and man. It is the kind of authority that can be exercised safely by both male and female who form the priesthood of believers, which receives delegated authority from Jesus Christ and the priestly calling of His body, the church.[9]

Genuine authority is exercised when it is recognized and authenticated as a gift in the church community. This authority is present in the person and readily accepted by the community for its own good.[10] Yet many women experience great difficulty in embracing the concepts of servanthood and authority, which appear to contradict each other. This dilemma is further accentuated by the teaching of Jesus Christ that being a leader primarily means being a servant to others.

Historically, male domination fostered the exclusion of women from both the secular and sacred spheres and undermined women's cultivation of the skills and intellect that are identified with leadership roles. This structure of domination is justified by a male supremacy that endorses men as the ones who really matter and women as existing in relation to men.[11] Men are regarded as powerful, active, self-sufficient, and fully human while women are viewed as weak, passive, and dependent. Male nature is human nature while woman nature is to be helpmeet to man.[12] Feminine qualities such as intuition, nurturing, and sensitivity are secondary, opposite, and negative in relation to so-called masculine qualities such as rationality.[13]

Complementarians support the views in the preceding paragraph by submitting that in terms of church leadership, it is the woman's responsibility to support male leadership, and in some cases, it is sinful for women to exercise leadership over men. This argument presupposes that males have the sole prerogative to exercise leadership authority in the church and segregates women in terms of the roles they should perform in the church.

Because of male domination in the church, some women experience difficulty in accepting positions of leadership. Morton noted that women have been conditioned all their lives to not seek positions of leadership. As a result, many of them who seek such positions are preconditioned to fail, although they may have the ability to succeed, because they are unable to assume the "man's way" without losing their integrity. Unequal salaries, promotion, and rank may dehumanize women. Morton also noted that in both seminaries and the church, males who are in control find it difficult or nearly impossible to accept women preachers.[14]

Parvey recognized the dilemma that women who have experienced a multiplicity of oppression, including racism, sexism, and classism are faced with. Although women know the rules and learn how to operate in these oppressive systems that bring special insights and claims to authority, these rules negate female authority because of their inability or unwillingness to recognize the wisdom or strength women have acquired through subordination. Women may fail to recognize the contribution they can make to their culture and to the body of Christ. They must be encouraged to claim authority to shoulder their responsibility in the church.[15]

Furthermore, because leadership stresses the paradoxical combination of servanthood and authority, women struggle to fully grasp this concept since they are accustomed to associate leadership with dominance and slavery with bondage. When leadership is viewed to mean authority over others, it overshadows the authenticity of authority as exercised in the body of Christ. Because women have been subjected to misused authority historically, either through abuse by slavery to men or to literal slavery, they are reluctant to embrace the slavery of true servanthood. The concept of leadership poses difficulty to women, even to those who have achieved authority over others. In order to grasp the real meaning of leadership, women must separate authority from dominance and slavery from bondage.[16]

Paul and the Use of Authority

In examining the meaning of the use of authority in Paul's writings, Liefield implied that the kind of authority prohibited to women in 1 Timothy 2:12, where Paul suffered not a woman to teach nor to usurp authority over the man but to be in silence, is not the normal kind of authority. The regular Greek word used for exercising authority, *exousiazō* was not the word used in this passage of scripture. Instead, a rare verb that appeared nowhere else in the New Testament, *authenteō* was used. In its earliest use, this verb was used to indicate violence, for example, "to murder," "to commit suicide," or "to project oneself sexually." In New Testament times, it was used to signify domination and a false claim to the right of initiating or originating something. In an attempt to understand why Paul used this rare verb, Paul's teachings must be examined in the context of the circumstances of his day. The circumstances that influenced Paul's writing of 1 Timothy and the other Pastoral Epistles were completely different from present-day circumstances.

Teaching and Authority

In 1 Timothy 2:11–15, Paul forbade women to teach or to usurp authority over men, but provided them the opportunity to learn, albeit in silence, which means that they were to sit in quiet submission as they were taught. For them to have been given permission to exercise this opportunity to learn was a departure from the norm of that time. It is not quite clear what historical situation in the Ephesian church caused Paul to give that instruction. One view expressed is that, because women were untrained and uneducated, they were more susceptible to false teaching and were not qualified to teach. Another view stated that women were victims of heresies that men taught them and that they were spreading these heresies within the church. Paul tried to prevent them from using the worship assembly for that purpose. There was also the belief that women might have been seeking to assert authority over men in the worship service.

Teachers were invested with a certain amount of authority to expound the word. Their students were obligated to listen to and obey their teaching.

The verb *didasko* is what was commonly used in connection with teaching in the New Testament and usually referred to public instruction or teaching of groups. A teacher was responsible for expounding the Word of God and for giving instructions in the Old Testament and apostolic teachings (1 Timothy 2:2; 2 Corinthians 4:17). In Paul's time, the culture of the Jewish society stipulated that a woman was not to exercise authority over a man. It is possible that Paul, in an attempt to introduce the Christian doctrine in a society that held strong cultural biases against women, made a culturally significant statement in 1 Timothy 2:11–15. Paul addressed women in general in the Ephesian congregation, and not only wives, even though he referred to the husband-wife relationship involving Adam and Eve. He focused on men and women as worshippers. Since false teaching was present within the church, he admonished women to submit to church elders who taught sound doctrine. Some of these false teachings might have come from recognized elders whom Paul was anxious to refute and to constrain through the preaching of sound doctrine. He was committed to promote godly living, behavior, and motives among the leaders and laity. Therefore, he advised Timothy to refute false teachers and to choose qualified church leaders.

He instructed women to learn in quiet submissiveness and forbade them to teach or exercise authority over men in the worship assembly. In dealing with the issue of teaching authority and submission, Paul referred to the pattern of creation to stress God's pattern of authority and submission, as it appeared that some women in the Ephesian worship assembly violated this pattern by teaching men. He drew on the rabbinic method of Old Testament interpretation to emphasize that the final authority rests with man by pointing out Adam's chronological primacy in creation.[17]

The following reasons are put forward as to why Paul forbade women to teach and to exercise authority over men, as well as to remain silent:

1. Women were victims of false teachers who took sexual advantage of them and might themselves have practiced false teachings (2 Timothy 3:6–7).
2. Women were uneducated and incapable of teaching.
3. Women were regarded as unreliable witnesses. Even though they were the first to have relayed the resurrection story, Paul did not regard them as witnesses (1 Corinthians 15).
4. The church was about to be inundated with early gnosticizing tendencies, such as the idea of the female principle on God and the

emphasis of Adam over Eve, possibly resulting in Paul's mentioning that Adam was first created (1 Timothy 2:13).
5. In the Greek culture, women were accepted as prophetesses but not as teachers (1 Corinthians 11; 1Timothy 2).
6. In the Jewish society, the teachers of scripture were revered and influential, which accounted for women not being accepted as teachers.

In her exegesis of 1 Timothy 2:11–15, Ann Bowman noted that Paul did not specially spell out the role of women in the worship assembly. Also, he did not discuss the teaching role of women within the worship assembly or in the larger ministry of the church in detail.[18] Although somewhat difficult to understand, this passage of scripture seems to be directed toward women in the church community at Ephesus who were influenced by false teachers. It must not be forgotten that the pastoral epistles, including 1 Timothy and 2 Timothy were written to guard against false teaching and heresy, which became the focus of about one-fifth of those epistles. The epistles to Timothy should therefore be viewed in the context of false teaching, even though they addressed other debated issues as well.

Paul made a similar reference in 2 Corinthians 11:3 where he was also concerned about seduction by false teachers. In 1 Corinthians 11:5, 14:26, Paul gave another brief explanation regarding the role of women in the worship assembly.[19] Then in 1 Corinthians 11:5, women were portrayed as praying and prophesying, which appears to have contradicted 1 Timothy 2:11–15, where women were prohibited from teaching men. However, the condition put forward in 1 Timothy 2:11–15 specifically applied to the Ephesian women who were influenced by false teachers to shirk their domestic responsibilities and to become disruptive and unproductive in the worship assembly. As a result, this passage of scripture could be viewed in cultural terms and should not be applied generally for the prohibition of teaching by women. What might have been the cultural norm for women, specifically the Ephesian women in Paul's day, may not be what a present-day culture is dictating.

As teaching entails a certain degree of authority, some people interpret Paul's writing to mean that the teaching ministry of women in the church should be limited since men have authority over women, and women should not teach men. Others contend that Paul limited women from having authority over men. In a more general context, some people believe that women should not be in positions of authority. Other people use Genesis 3:16 that speaks of the husband ruling over the wife to validate their argument against women being in positions of authority. Although a husband's authority over his wife and entire family is absolute and ordained by God, it does not prevent his wife from assuming a leadership role within the church, including the role of pastor. Regardless of whatever role the wife performs within the church, it does not negate the husband's authority over her. With regard to the role of teaching, the Holy Spirit endows both men and women with the spiritual gift of teaching. It is He who reveals the Word of God to teachers and gives them the ability to expound the truth effectively to others.

Liefield pointed out that the teaching that was prohibited to women in 1 Timothy did not involve the expounding of biblical texts because the Bible was not yet completed or widespread. Instead, it meant the transmission of the apostolic tradition. The authoritative teachings of Jesus Christ and the Apostles were first transmitted orally before they were written in the New Testament and were not accepted from the mouths of women.

Clearly, the authority that was invested solely in men to transmit the apostolic tradition before the completion of the Bible no longer exists because the scripture is now the final authority upon which the church stands.[20] Authority that previously resided in the messenger is now superseded by the message of the written word, a fact that supports the role of women in exercising authority. Both men and women must rely on the Holy Spirit in whom the power of the Gospel rests. Since the power of the Gospel does not lie within an individual, men and women can be equally efficient in spreading the Gospel with similar results. As a result, women were very active in spreading the Gospel during Paul's ministry, which suggests that Paul did not restrict women's role in teaching as a general Christian doctrine.

Authority in Today's Context

Liefield contended that the authority Paul forbade women to exercise over men was different from ecclesiastical authority based on several reasons. Firstly, ordination does not confer authority of one person over another. Secondly, the ultimate authority under God does not lie with a person. Thirdly, ministry emphasizes service, not the exercising of authority. Lastly, the reference to authority in 1 Timothy is considered difficult to understand but does not pose a hindrance to the normal ministries of women.[21]

R. T. France affirmed that Paul's reference to a woman not exercising authority over a man was in connection with the husband-wife relationship in the context of marriage rather than in the general context of the relation between man and woman. In 1 Timothy 2:12–15, Paul alluded to the story of Adam and Eve, a married couple, and to the issue of childbearing, a distinctive role of a wife. Hence, it is safe to conclude that the focus of this chapter was on the proper role of a wife in relation to her husband in the context of worship.[22] This being so, France's interpretation bears significant implications when viewed in terms of the performance of roles by men and women within the church, outside the confines of marriage.

In forbidding women to teach, Paul stressed their need to learn first (1 Timothy 2:11), contrary to the order of his day that fostered male learning. According to the rabbis and many theologians, women were considered unsuitable for teaching based on their mental and moral inferiority, and as a result, women were not taught the Torah. The lack of learning rendered women incapable of teaching. Paul's desire for women to learn opened the door to speculative argument as to whether Paul intended women to teach or considered it inappropriate for them to do so once they learned. It is logical to conclude that, outside the issues that prevailed within the church at Ephesus on which Paul's Epistle to Timothy focused, there is much room for debate over the precluding of women from exercising authority over men.[23]

In addition, proponents of the view that women should not exercise authority over men are convinced that their view rings true in the ecclesiastical realm and may vigorously oppose the ordination of women. However, they lose sight of the fact that women exercise authority in other areas of teaching in the ministry. Outside ordained ministry, women are school and university teachers, Sunday school teachers, and Bible class teachers. They assume the primary responsibility for missionary outreach and church building in some areas of the world. Women teach men in these situations. Even in the secular realm, a large percentage of women are in teaching positions. The question then arises as to why the interpretation of Paul's writings pertaining to the issue of authority should be confined to ordained ministry.

Authoritative Concept of Office in the New Testament in the Post-Pauline Church and in the Present-Day Church

Some proponents link the issue of silence and teaching in 1 Timothy 2:12 with the priestly or pastoral office, which seemingly bears an authoritative concept and precludes women from participating in the ministry of proclaiming the Word of God. With regard to the authoritative concept of office, various denominations hold different views. For example, in churches where the congregations are invested in all forms of ministry, such as the Congregationalists, Quakers, and the Salvation Army, men and women enjoy relative equality in profession and status. The Anglican denomination focuses on the positions and activities of women and disapproves the ordination of women even though women are allowed to teach and preach in most evangelical Anglican Churches. The crux of the problem arises in the priestly office. Although large parts of the Eucharist may be delegated to other members of the congregation, including women, the Eucharist prayer and the breaking of the bread may be reserved for male priests only. However, even the Anglican denomination is slowly opening its doors to female priests. This denomination allows women to be deacons and to preach because a deacon is considered a subordinate officer to a priest who is in charge of a parish or a group of parishes. A woman is allowed to preach and teach under the delegation and authority of a male incumbent.[24] The Lutheran and the Reformed Churches are not quite clear on the position of women, especially in terms of their ministry in proclaiming the Word.

Throughout the ages, the authoritative concept of the priestly office assumed different meanings and functions. Under the old covenant in Israel, only men of the Tribe of Levi could be called to the priestly office since only the High Priest could enter the Holy of Holies within the tabernacle to present the sacrifice of atonement on the altar. In the Middle Ages, the priest was regarded as a mediator of divine grace and as the representative of Christ. Currently, in their Mass, Roman Catholics still believe that the sacramental, consecrated priestly office should be open only to men and that the priest is endowed with the authority to continue the priestly office of Christ.

However, after Jesus Christ made the atonement for the sin of the world on Mount Calvary, the priestly office based on the old covenant was erased when Jesus Christ became the eternal High Priest after the order of Melchizedek (Hebrews 7:17), not after the order of Levi as was the case under the old covenant. With the advent of the church era and in the New Testament, Jesus Christ alone bears the office of priest. He is the only officiator and celebrant of the liturgy.

In light of the proclamation of the office of Christ as High Priest, the reformed concept of "priesthood of believers" emerged (1 Peter 2:9). The reformed concept of office, meaning "service and ministry," came with it. To this end, all members of the body of Christ are called based on the gifts that the Holy Spirit bestows upon them. Jesus Christ is the one who builds His church and the gates of hell shall not prevail against it. The call to humble service should assist women in carving out a niche for themselves in ministry as they respect the gifts of other members of the body of Christ and allow others to minister with their respective gifts. As women endeavor to stress their service rather than the offices entrusted upon them by God, they struggle with the task of harmonizing their ministry with their position as women in performing a "clerical office" shaped by men in a particular way.[25] It is important for women to lift up the name of Jesus Christ and to labor in building the church by example and by proclaiming the unadulterated Word of God.

The Meaning of *Headship* and Authority in Paul's Writings

In the context of human relationships, Paul used *head* to mean authority. In 1 Corinthians 11:3, Paul stated that Christ is the head of every man and the man is the head of the woman and God is the head of Christ. In Ephesians 5:21–25, he exhorted wives to be subject to their own husbands as to the Lord, for the husband is the head of the wife as Christ also is the head of the church. Furthermore, husbands and wives were to submit to each other in the fear of the Lord. Husbands were to love their wives as Christ loved the church and gave Himself for it.

This passage of scripture in Ephesians 5 describes Jesus Christ as being the head of the entire mystical body, the church, which includes men and women. As head of his wife, the husband must shoulder a special responsibility before God for himself, his wife, and children. Paul compared the husband-and-wife relationship to the relationship between God the Father and God the Son. Jesus Christ was fully God and was equal with His Father, yet He willingly submitted to the will of His Father (Philippians 2:5; Colossians 2:9–10; John 8:28–29, 14:28, 31). Likewise, men and women are equal before God even though women must submit to their husbands. This submission does not imply that the wife is inferior to her husband, similarly to how Jesus Christ was not inferior to His Father.

Like Complementarians, von Kirschbaum contended that it is an undisputed fact that man as head of woman is still valid in the church. The headship of man over woman was not the result of sin but was the order that was present from the beginning of time just as how woman was man's "helper."[26] Complementarians subscribe to the argument that if God has sanctioned male headship in the home, then this headship concept is also applicable to the church. On the other hand, Egalitarians support the headship of man in the home but do not subscribe to sole male headship in the church. They argue that women should have equal opportunity to exercise leadership gifts like men in the church and that there should not only be male church leaders as the head or authority and as overseers over women in leadership positions.

Paul used the Greek word *kephale*, the physical head, the part of one's body to describe the husband as head of the wife. This Greek word was also used to mean "forward" as one who leads, but not in the sense of *director*. It means foremost in terms of position. *Kephale* was also used for someone who went before the troops into battle. Paul did not choose the word *arche* that meant "boss." Neither did he choose the word *rosh* that meant both "physical head" and "ruler." The husband is before his wife in terms of position. He leads the way by being in front and may be regarded as the one who sticks his neck out for and is the physical protector of the family. This position does not recognize the husband as the boss or controller or as being superior to his wife. He is the head of his wife in terms of respecting, loving, and caring for her. In turn, she respectfully submits to his headship that also extends to his household.

Paul patterned his new model of Christian marriage after the relationship of Christ and the church. It reflected an egalitarian style rather than a patriarchal style and was a radical departure from marriage of his day. At that time, as was previously mentioned, women were considered to be inferior or as a distraction to men. A husband did not respect the needs and feelings of his wife who was not privy to the needs of her husband. In reality, Paul opposed the entrenched Greek philosophy of men-and-women relationships. Paul introduced equality in the relationship of a husband and wife in which they could be regarded as equal partners. This relationship demonstrated an aura of togetherness in which love, submission, and care were reciprocated between the partners (1 Peter 3:1–2, 7).

Headship in Paul's writing must be viewed theologically as deriving its meaning from "God is the head of Christ," which does not speak of authority but of equality and oneness in being. Olsen pointed out that 1 Corinthians 7:3–4 signifies complete mutuality and that *headship* manifests caring love in representative responsibility and sacrificial service (John 3:16). First Corinthians 11:3 speaks of the representative nature of Christ's headship. Because of serving in love and exercising sacrificial authority, Christ became "the top," "the first," "the head of man and the church" (Ephesians 1:22–23; Colossians 1:8). Olsen contended that headship in the context of man and woman does not signify "the top" or "the first" of a hierarchical structure but is representative and speaks of an organic unity. In his representative position as head, man must display a relationship with God as that demonstrated by Christ on earth to bring glory to God so that woman in turn may bring honor to man who is the representative head.

Some people maintain that male headship was present in the Garden of Eden because Adam was first created and the woman was created for the man (1 Corinthians 11:8–9). Adam demonstrated this form of headship to Eve in a similar manner as defined by Olsen. The relationship that Adam and Eve shared with each other was void of Adam exercising authority over Eve. Instead, their relationship was one of shared dominion in which they were commissioned to "fill the earth and subdue it" and oneness in which man became complete with woman (Genesis 1:27). After the fall, both the vertical relationship Adam and Eve had with God and the horizontal relationship between Adam and Eve were broken.[27] Not only did Adam and Eve cease to share dominion over God's creation, but in exercising his headship, Adam began to "rule over" (Genesis 3:16) or to "dominate" Eve. Adam assumed authority over Eve by naming her in terms of her biological role of bearing children (Genesis 3:20), which was the beginning of male domination within the family system.

In his analysis of the context of 1 Corinthians 11:3, Culver offered a traditional view regarding the principle of headship in this passage. He stated that headship is a common metaphor for authority. It does not symbolize source because God is not the source of Christ. He argued that the Christian man's head is Christ, and the Christian woman's head is the man as also the head of Christ is God, thus removing the meaning of this passage from the home and marriage relationship and applying it in the context of the church. He argued that Paul, in referring to the laws of creation, treated the first man and woman as archetypes. Each was viewed not only as husband or wife, but as either "manness or womanness forever." Hence the Genesis account referred to the male and female humanity in the church. Because woman was derived from man (1 Corinthians 11:9), Paul implied some kind of precedence to man (over woman) in public church relations.[28]

Grenz and Kjesbo noted that headship involves both authority and obedience that Jesus Christ expressed to His Father.[29] The exercising of this headship does not present man as boss and woman as subordinate.[30] Olsen stressed that even though man may serve as the symbol of authority within the context of the church, when Paul spoke of man-woman relationship, he spoke of complete equality in the new creation (2 Corinthians 5:17). Man and woman are one. Woman would negate her own existence by separating herself from the body of man from whence she was taken, and man who was born of woman can only appear before God with woman.[31]

When operating in the context of Christian freedom and the church, there is no justification for women not to exercise authority in the use of their gifts in the body of Christ. A study paper on "Women in Ministry" for New York Mennonite Conference approved in August 1992 shed some very thoughtful and interesting light on the concept of the exercising of headship within the context of the church. This paper maintained that if the concept of headship is understood correctly, it permits the inclusion of women in every sphere of church life to function according to the divine pattern. It pointed out that God exercised headship over Christ by placing Him at the right hand of His throne (Ephesians 1:19–23; 1 Peter 3:22). God helped Jesus Christ to exercise the authority that belonged to the head rather than prevented Him from doing so. In the church, Jesus Christ exercises authority in a similar fashion where He gives gifts to the church. These gifts nurture and build up the church. The church grows from Jesus Christ as its head (Ephesians 4:15–16; Colossians 2:19) so that it can become mature and attain to the whole measure of the fullness of Christ (Ephesians 4:13, 15). In Paul's description of Christ as head of the church, he downplayed the component of "rule" and stressed that of "nurture." (Ephesians 5:25–27). Jesus Christ has assumed the responsibility for nurturing and grooming His bride in preparation for her ultimate reign with Him (2 Timothy 2:12; Revelation 5:10, 22:5).

In understanding headship as being *nurture*, the study paper identified two characteristics, which are authority and the source of growth. If male headship within the church were to demonstrate nurture, a male church leader may include a gifted woman alongside him on a leadership team, initially mentoring her and imparting to her the skills and wisdom to fully attain her spiritual gifts. As the woman gains experience, the male church leader will empower her to assume responsibility for an out-front leadership role and even place himself in a position where he can benefit from her gifts. A complementary team in which each member contributes his or her uniqueness and one in which responsibilities are assigned according to abilities and not gender will emerge.[32]

Power

The matter of humble servant must be stressed if the exercising of power in leadership style within the church is to be understood in its true perspective. Today, many people understand leadership as the exercise of power by someone over others by promoting one's views, program, or agenda.[33] This concept of leadership embraces the male dominance theory that impedes the right of women to exercise power and authority over men. Jesus Christ clearly taught that being a leader means being the servant of all (Mark 10:44).

There are different kinds of power that have been identified by several authors, but the one that is emphasized in this chapter is the anointed power that is imparted to the body of Christ by God the Holy Spirit for service in whatever areas of ministry to which God has called members of His body. The Holy Spirit is the source of power (Luke 1:34). It is He who endured the disciples with power on the Day of Pentecost to go forth and preach with boldness and authority.

As a man, Jesus Christ needed to be endued with power before He started His earthly ministry. The Spirit led Him in the wilderness where He remained for forty days and was tempted by the devil. At the end of this season of fasting and praying, Jesus Christ emerged triumphant and in the power of the Spirit to carry out the ministry which He was sent to perform (Luke 4; Matthew 4). Jesus Christ also retreated to solitary places to pray to His Father in heaven in order to receive strength and power for His ministry (Mark 1:35). He also imparted His example to His disciples before sending them to minister. He gave them power and authority over all devils and to cure diseases (Luke 9:1) and power to tread on serpents and scorpions and over all the power of the enemy (Luke 10:19). On the eve of His return to His Father in heaven, He delegated His power to the eleven apostles in the Great Commission (Matthew 28:18–20).

In order to be successful in ministry, people must surrender themselves to the Holy Spirit who is the "Comforter, Teacher, Counselor and Guardian, and the one who gives the enabling power."[34]

Good and Evil Use of Power

Power may be defined as the ability to cause or prevent change.[35] It fosters personhood and promotes independent choice and action. Power may be exercised either in a good way or in an evil way. When used in an evil manner, it is applied as domination that is detrimental to liberating others to organize their creative capabilities and contributions for their own and for the common good. The dominant person enforces his will on his subordinates whom he coerces into serving his end. The exercising of such power prevents self-definition. In the case of male domination, Carroll noted that women are excluded from public and sacred spaces and are hindered from cultivating skills and intellect that are linked with leadership roles.[36]

Although power has been viewed as possessing control over others, participants of the World Council of Churches Conference in Sheffield, England, in 1981, felt that if exercised correctly, power is the ability to implement action, to bring about an effect, sometimes a change.[37] Once it is exercised, power does not produce a static effect, but energizes and mobilizes.

Isasi-Díaz endorsed this opinion by defining power as the ability to enable all persons to become the most they can be. In order to understand power, relational structures and operational modes in all spheres of life must be established to promote and facilitate the self-realization of all persons. The creativity of all persons should be promoted so that they can contribute to the common good.[38] Isasi-Díaz noted serious difficulties for women to exercise power, both in the secular and spiritual arenas. In the Judeo-Christian context, women were excluded from the public and religious spheres, especially those whose male headship was religiously legitimized.[39] This exclusion permitted little testing of their presence and power even though they could effectively impinge on male power.[40] Men's fear of women's sexual power was identified as a cause for this attitude toward women.

During the fourth century, through its bishops and Episcopal Synods, the church gradually exercised the authority to control "unclean" power. The Christian understanding of properly ordered power was influenced by ancient medicine that taught that women were less formed and ordered than men and stressed the irrational nature of women and the intrinsic pollution of disorderly female power as compared with the rational explicit power of male being and order.[41]

In her views about the framework of earthly order, von Kirschbaum identified man as the bearer of power as he is regarded as the "head." However, Jesus Christ, the all-powerful, is the head of every man, and His power is the foundation and limitation of all other power. Therefore, for power to be appropriately and effectively exercised, man must acknowledge Jesus Christ as head and be subjected to Him in the same manner in which Jesus Christ was obedient to and subjected to His Father who is His head. Jesus Christ set the model of obedience and subjection for women to follow and determines the highest position of men.[42] Therefore, in exercising power, people must do so through loving, visioning, listening, and challenging in the power of the Holy Spirit and must accept others. Their desire for power must die.

Women have been ambivalent about claiming and exercising power in Christianity, which Paul aptly described when he reminded us that God's strength is made perfect in weakness. He was enthused with his infirmities in order to obtain the power of Christ (2 Corinthians 12:9). In their weak and powerless state, women are actually in an advantageous position to accept and impart the gift of love that God bestows upon them and empowers them through the Holy Spirit to show to others. The feminine traits of submission and powerlessness can be regarded as effective agents and vibrant assets in accomplishing this purpose. The masculine traits of authority and power can be regarded as ineffective agents, especially if there is the presence of a strong desire to exercise this authority and power over others, which is alien to the Holy Spirit.[43]

Since power involves the right of authority to use power, it is very important to understand the appropriate use of power as it applies to ministry. Rollo May identified five uses of power, namely exploitative, manipulative, competitive, nutrient, and integrating. Exploitative power subjects people to being used by the one who holds the power. Competitive power involves one person "going up" because another person has "gone down." Manipulative power is present when someone uses another person's desperation or anxiety to take advantage over that person. These three uses of power cannot be applied appropriately in the body of Christ where each member is important, and his or her participation is crucial for the healthy functioning of the entire body. May identified the other two uses of power, namely, nutrient and integrating power, as appropriately applicable to the church. Nutrient power is power for the other person, and integrative power is power with the other person.[44] These two types of power are exercised as a result of the authority that is bestowed upon someone in leadership position, which the members of a community grant to that person and which is used for the benefit of that community.

Should women be excluded from exercising these two types of leadership power? The answer to this question lies in the fact that God the Holy Spirit empowers whom He will to exalt those persons to leadership positions.

He empowers both males and females and endows them with the gift of leadership, which is sanctioned by the church community. Jesus Christ set the example for the appropriate and proper use of power in ministering to the needs of others and in serving others. His example is the only one to follow and to promote. Because of their leadership styles, women are capable of wielding both nutrient and integrative power appropriately in the church once the Holy Spirit leads them. In chapter 7, the leadership styles of women are discussed in greater detail.

Submission

On the matter of submission, some people view this concept to mean that people are to obey those to whom they submit or that the persons to whom they submit have control over them. In Genesis 18:12 and 1 Peter 3:16 where Sarah was referred to as calling her husband Abraham lord, she specifically rendered due respect to him as her husband and as head of the household. Submission referred to in Ephesians 5:21–24 is twofold. It exhorts us to submit to each other in the fear of God and wives to submit to their husbands as to the Lord. The concept of submission must be understood in the context of Christ's relationship to His body, the church. Paul viewed submission in the context of love and respect. Christians submit to Jesus Christ as the head of the church, cognizant of the fact the Jesus Christ died for them, loves and cares for them. Similarly, wives should submit to their husbands, fully assured that their husbands love and care for them and that they will be willing to represent them if necessary. Husbands are not expected to demand submission from their wives or to use it as a means to control their wives.

To submit "is to recognize your place within the God-given order of Society and to act appropriately to that place, by accepting the authority of those to whom God has entrusted it."[45] In this section, two important models of submission will be the focus of discussion. These are the dominance and submission model and the mutual submissive model. Traditionalists, Complementarians, and Egalitarians use these models to support male-female relationships. In his examination of the issue of submission, France stated that submission must be viewed within the context of the order that God has designed for human society at different levels. Within this order, each person should perform a specific role. Although submission is usually considered as a feminine trait, Jesus Christ submitted to the will of His Father to fulfill the plan of salvation. It is crucial to note, however, that both the feminine trait of submission and the masculine trait of aggressiveness can be considered God-given strengths. Christians who walk in the Spirit can possess both of these strengths. The world understands submissiveness as demonstrated weakness and as a lack of spirit but recognizes that Jesus Christ applied both submissiveness and aggression to overcome the world. Christians ought to possess the qualities that Jesus Christ possessed and use them when necessary.[46]

The Dominance and Submission Model

Traditionalists and Complementarians use this model. They use the obedience of Jesus Christ to His Father as the basis for the subordination of women to men in general and of wife to husband in particular. They regard the authority that flows from the Father to the Son as linear and view all human relationships likewise. Males exercise authority over females in a linear fashion. They argue that women should voluntarily submit themselves to male leadership as Jesus Christ voluntarily submitted Himself to the will of His Father. They support this argument on the basis that female submission does not mean female inferiority, that a female simply exercises a different role from a male.[47] However, the functional submission of Jesus Christ to His Father's will does not entail any ontological subordination. Jesus Christ voluntarily chose to become human for a specific reason. His was a redemptive subordination that applies to the functional differences among Christians. His example of voluntarily laying aside the splendors of heaven to become first and foremost human and to suffer death on the cross is worthy to be noted by Christians and is to be their influence when relating to God and developing proper attitudes toward one another. The example set by Jesus Christ lends credence to the functional differences that become evident when the Holy Spirit calls people to specific areas of service and endows them with specific spiritual gifts to carry out those areas of service, irrespective of gender. Those who are called to leadership are by no means ontologically superior to others who serve in subordinate roles even though the scriptures exhort us to submit to those who are called to leadership.

Complementarians do not subscribe to the view that some people must submit to others based on spiritual gifts. Instead, they use the basis of gender for justifying why all women should submit to all men. They erroneously equate biologically determined differences in gender with functional differences resulting from the call of the Holy Spirit on people's lives and spiritual gifts.⁴⁸ Their position defeats the very reason why Jesus Christ was revealed in the flesh mainly as human rather than as male. It works at cross purposes with the refusal of Jesus Christ to participate in the stigma of dehumanizing women, thus undermining the promulgation of the dominance and submission model.

This model is foreign to the ideals of submission in the context of the church and to the relationship of male and female in general and of husband and wife specifically. There was no dominance and submission in the relationship of Adam and Eve before the fall when God gave them equal dominion over every other living thing and to subdue the earth (Genesis 1:28). Equal dominion suggests togetherness and a unilateral and functional equality. In fact, Genesis 2:23–24 stresses oneness by identifying the female as woman (*ishshah*), taken from man (*ish*), and by presenting this as the reason for man leaving his parents and cleaving to his wife and the two becoming one flesh.

The dominance and submission model emerged after the fall when the harmonious relationships of man with God and man with woman were severely affected, and the equilibrium in nature was shaken. Genesis 3:14–19 vividly describes the quality of human life after the fall.⁴⁹ Man was to rule over his wife. This shift in man and woman relationship is used by Complementarians as the prescription for supporting the dominance and submission model. However, this model breathes manipulation, patriarchy, and destruction. It allows Christian husbands to wield unhealthy power over their wives and male leaders to exert dominance over female leaders in ministry. It crushes the wills and spirits of women to scale greater heights and to plunge into deeper depths in serving God. It enmeshes them in a destructive and vicious web spun by societal norms for centuries.

In his study on sexism and the human personality, Richard D. Kahoe, Chairman of the Psychology Department of Georgetown College, concluded that it is psychologically unhealthy for men and women to accept female subordination. Within the framework of the dominance and submission model, he described men who oppose equality (of man and woman) as having the tendency to be more authoritarian and nonconfirming. On the other hand, conventional submissive women tend to be maladjusted, resistant to change, self-protective, and risk avoiding. Moreover, there is a strong likelihood that the male-female relationship that operates under this model is also unhealthy.⁵⁰

The Mutual Submissive Model

This model emphasizes an understanding of humanity and of male-female relations in which humanity is regarded as filial and in which male and female who were created in the image of God find their true being in communion and mutual personal relations of love. In His humanity, Jesus Christ had a threefold relation of communion, mutual indwelling, and "perichoretic" unity with His Father.[51] Although He willingly submitted Himself to His Father's will, the Trinity presents a balanced model as it portrays mutual dependence between the Father and the Son.

This mutual dependence is the key concept that should apply to the church community where man and woman should be mutually dependent on one another and should be allowed to participate at all levels in the church community. This includes the performance of leadership roles by women. It is of paramount importance that women should participate in the life of the church. There are no fixed or defined roles for man or woman in the church based on their genders, such as male leading and women following or submitting to male leadership only. Neither is there a place for female dominance in the home or in the church as it undermines the male-female relationship. More importantly, there is no place for dominance among males and females in ministry where the Holy Spirit calls some people to positions of leadership.

A good understanding of male-female relations would reveal the primary purpose of God for humanity as filial where male and female find their true being in communion with God and with each other and in mutual personal relations of love. Humans are drawn by the Spirit to share in Christ's communion with His Father. The male-female relations ought to be viewed in terms of man's union with God in Christ and (in terms of) caring love, mutual functioning complementarity, and mutual submission.[52]

Contrary to the dominance and submission model, which breathes patriarchy and a fixed mode of male-female relations in which women have relinquished their wills by accommodating the wills of their husbands and fathers and which results in some cases to women being crushed, to their fighting back, or to their learning to become "subtly undercutting and slyly manipulative,"[53] the mutual submissive model presents a healthier male-female relationship of mutual submission under God who is both transcendent and immanent and is within and without us as noted in Ephesians 4:6, which states, "One God and Father of all, who is over all and through all, and in all." As a result, male and female can live in God and vice versa if they live in mutual service and mutual submission. Mollenkot stated that mutual submission and mutual service of male and female are the best road to psychological health and positive human relationships. Christians are able to experience harmony through mutual submission and mutual service as a result of yielding their internal willpower to the will of Almighty God.

Ephesians 5:21 clearly endorses the mutual submissive model as Christians are exhorted to submit to one another out of reverence for Christ. Failure to submit to one another and to serve one another can result in mutual destruction (Galatians 5:13–15). This mutual destruction is the tale of woe in many male-female relationships.

The story of the incarnation of Christ epitomizes mutual service, mutual submission, and the fusing of Christ's will with a universal divine will, which resulted in the intertwining and oneness between God the Father and God the Son. The submission of Jesus to His Father's will provides the ideal for the manner in which human beings should relate to God and to one another. The mutual submissive model shows Christ in the flesh surrendering Himself for the church in sacrificial love on the cross and the church submitting to Him in return for dying to redeem the church. It is not viewed as a model of a woman's submission to her husband but more fittingly applies to the model for Christian husbands to follow in loving their wives just as how Christ loved the church and gave himself for it (Ephesians 5:25). A man must treat his wife with self-giving concern and respect. In turn, the wife should emulate the church's submissive response to the self-sacrifice of Christ and respond with respect and deference toward her husband.[54] This is the ideal model for the Christian husband and wife and for the male-female Christian relationship.

This model of submission of Jesus Christ to His Father and the mutual dependence between the Father and the Son are the yardsticks for measuring human relationships. Not only is it crucial for male and female to submit to each other in the body of Christ, but it is equally imperative for their mutual dependence to be operative at all levels of the church community where leadership roles for women should be encouraged and fostered.

1. Alice L. Hageman, ed., *Sexist Religion and Women in the Church: No More Silence!* (New York: Association Press, 1974), 48.
2. John C. B. and Ellen Low Webster, eds., *The Church and Women in the Third World* (Philadelphia: The Westminster Press,1985), in from Constance F. Parvey, "Third World Women and Men: Effects of Cultural Change on Interpretation of Scripture," 105–106.
3. Stanley Grenz with Denise Muir Kjesbo, *Women in the Church: A Biblical Theology of Women in Ministry* (Downers Grove, Illinois: InterVarsity Press, 1995), 215.
4. Hageman, op. cit., 48–49.
5. Grenz with Kjesbo, op. cit., 200–205.
6. Clare Benedicks Fischer, Betsy Brenneman, and Anne McGrew Bennett, *Women in a Strange Land: Search for a New Image* (Philadelphia: Fortress Press, 1975), in Karen L. Bloomquist, "We as Ministers, AMEN!" 75.
7. Grenz with Kjesbo, op. cit., 203–205.
8. Constance Parvey, ed., *The Community of Women and men in the Church* (Geneva: The World Council of Churches, 1983), 116–117.
9. Myrtle Langley, *Equal Woman: A Christian Feminist Perspective* (UK: Marshall, Morgan and Scott, 1983), 177–178.
10. Parvey, op. cit., 134.
11. Virgil Elizondo and Norbert Greinacher, eds., *Women in a Men's Church* (New York: The Seabury Press, 1980), 46, in M. French, *The Women's Room* (New York:, 1978), 289, in Elizabeth Carroll, "Can Male Domination Be Overcome?"
12. Ibid., in C. C. Gould and M. W. Wartofsky, *Women and Philosophy* (New York: 1976), 192.
13. Ibid., in C. C. Gould and M. W. Wartofsky, ibid., 263, 23.
14. Hageman, op. cit., 37.
15. Parvey, op. cit., 133.
16. Carol E. Becker, *Leading Women: How the Church Can Avoid Leadership Traps and Negotiate the Gender Maze* (Nashville: Abingdon Press, 1996), 23–24.
17. Ann L. Bowman, "Women in Ministry: An Exegetical Study of 1 Timothy 2:11–15, *International School of Theology*" (Spring 1992) [Online] Available http.//www.leaderu.com/isot/docs/womenmin.html (03/04/2001), 6–9.
18. Ibid., 2.
19. "Policy on Women in Ministry" [Online] Available http.//www.covchurch.org/cov/html/women_in_min.html (22/04/2001), 4.
20. Bonnidell Clouse and Robert G. Clouse, eds., *Women in Ministry: Four Views* (Downers Grove, Illinois 60515: InterVarsity Press, 1989), in from Walter L. Liefield, "A Plural Ministry View: Your Sons and Your Daughters Shall Prophesy," 147–151.
21. Ibid., 149–150.
22. R. T. France, *Women in the Church's Ministry: A Text Case for Biblical Interpretation* (Grand Rapids, Michigan: William B. Eerdmans Publishing Company, 1995), 61
23. Dorothy Pape, *In Search of God's Ideal Woman: A Personal Examination of the New Testament* (Downers Grove, Illinois 60515, 1976), 187–188.
24. R. T. France, op. cit., 29–32.
25. Eleanor Jackson, ed., *The Question of Woman: The Collected Writings of Charlotte*

von Kirschbaum, trans. John Shepherd (Grand Rapids, Michigan/Cambridge, UK: William B. Eerdmans Publishing Company, 1944), 173–184.
26. Ibid., 103–104.
27. Norskov V. Olsen, *The New Relatedness for Man & Woman in Christ: A Mirror of the Divine* (Loma Linda, California: 1993), 107–112.
28. Clouse and Clouse, op. cit., in Robert D. Culver, "A Traditional View: Let Your Women Keep Silence," 30–31.
29. Grenz with Kjesbo, op. cit., 152.
30. Pape, op. cit., 164.
31. Jackson, op. cit., 104–107.
32. Women in Ministry: A Study Paper for New York Mennonite Conference [Online] Available http.//freenet.buffalo.edu/-nymennon/womenmin.htm (22/04/2001), 7–8.
33. Grenz with Kjesbo, op. cit., 216.
34. Faith B. Abijola, *The Galilean Women of Today* (Ibadan, Feyisetan Press, 1998), 33–36.
35. Grenz with Kjesbo, op. cit., 225, from Rollo May, *Power and Innocence: A Search for the Sources of Violence* (New York: W. W. Norton, 1972), 99.
36. Elizondo and Greinacher, op. cit., 45–46.
37. Parvey, op. cit., 133.
38. Nantawan Boonprasat Lewis, et al, *Sisters Struggling in the Spirit: A Woman of Color Theological Anthropology* (Louisville, Kentucky: Women Ministries Program Area, National Ministries Division, Presbyterian Church, 1994), cited from Ada Maria Isasi-Diaz, "Mujeristas: A Name of Our Own," 134–135; Isabel Allende, *The House of the Spirits* (New York: Knof, 1985), 358–368.
39. Kim Power, *Veiled Desire: Augustine on Women* (New York, New York, 10017: The Continuum Publishing Company, 1995), 66, in Douglas, *Purity* 5. 35.
40. Ibid., in Douglas, *Purity*, 104.
41. Ibid., 67.
42. Jackson, op. cit., 100–101.
43. Clare Fischer, Betsy Brenneman, and Anne McGrew Bennett, *Women in a Strange Land: Search for a New Image* (Philadelphia: Fortress Press, 1975), 96.
44. Ibid.
45. R. T. France, op. cit., 34.
46. Leadership, Power and Submission, cited from Betty Miller, "What Does the Bible Say about Women in Ministry?" [Online] Available www.bible.com, 3
47. Virginia Ramsey Mollenkot, *Women, Men and the Bible*, rev. ed. with Study Guide (New York: Crossroad, 1988), 102.
48. Grenz with Kjesbo, op. cit., 152–153.
49. Mollenkot, op. cit., 111.
50. Ibid., 115
51. Olsen, op. cit., 16–17.
52. Ibid.
53. Mollenkot, op. cit., 105.
54. Ibid., 103–113

Chapter Three:
Women Leaders in Old and New Testament Times

Women Leaders in the Old Testament

The Bible clearly demonstrates that God's divine pattern and order for humanity provide for the prominent and significant contribution of women in society throughout the ages. The correlation between the complementary and interdependence of the two sexes is evident and inevitable. Some Old Testament texts that support this premise are Genesis 1:26–28, which states that both male and female were created in the image of God and were given dominion, and Exodus 38:8 and 1 Samuel 2:1–10, which reveal that women participated in Israel's worship.

Although the ministry of women is primarily a New Testament phenomenon, the leadership roles performed by some women of distinction in the Old Testament provide the basis for women in ministry. There were prophetesses, judges, and queens among the women of distinction. Although the politics of public life remained almost exclusively male in the Hebrew society and the virtuous wife watched over the affairs of her household (Proverbs 21:23), occasionally, women did assume authority. Although kings usually reigned over Israel during the monarchy, occasionally, queens functioned as heads of state (2 Kings 11:3). There were also wise women who wielded tremendous influence in public life (1 Samuel 14:1–20, 20:16–22).

The status of women in the ancient community of faith was overshadowed by a patriarchal family structure that promoted male dominance in the public life of Israel. Jewish laws protected husbands and families by ensuring legitimate male heirs to whom the promise that conditioned the existence of Israel could be passed on. The family name lived on through the sons, whereas a married woman relinquished her family of origin for her husband's family. Women were viewed in the framework of marriage as wives, mothers, and mistresses of households. Women were to function as "fruitful" wives, and barrenness was frowned upon (Exodus 23:25–26; 1 Samuel 1:1, 2:1; Job 24:21; Psalm 113:9). Men were regarded as the progenitors and women as the child bearers, subjecting them to a subordinate and restricting position. An adult woman lived under the authority of her nearest male relative. Her husband or her father could cancel her vow to God (Numbers 30:3–16). Her husband could divorce her, but not vice versa (Deuteronomy 24:1–4).

Women were not educated as the Rabbis prevented all women, both married and single, from studying the scripture and the law to safeguard their diversion from their binding maternal role. Women were regarded as temptations to sin. No respectable women participated in public life but spent the majority of their lives within the confines of their homes. Despite this fact, some women occasionally assumed the lead role outside of their homes, for example, Abigail, who intervened on her foolish husband's behalf (1 Samuel 25:2–35). Some women frequently engaged in commerce (Proverbs 31:13–18). Women were not included in the number of persons needed to have a synagogue, and their testimony was not accepted in a court of law.[1] There were no women priests as the Torah stipulated that only men could serve as priests although there was no theoretical or theological explanation regarding the reasons for excluding women from the priesthood.[2] Grenz and Kjesbo cited some possible reasons that scholars have identified for this exclusion. One such reason is that women might have found it difficult to function as priests while performing the maternal role. Another explanation was that women could not perform the work that involved the sacrificial system, such as killing and lifting heavy animals. Thirdly, there was a theological reason that could have been prompted by the struggle against Canaanite fertility cults in which female priests served as prostitutes. Only the Levites, male descendents of Aaron, could become priests.

Despite the male priesthood, women participated in Israelite worship since God had covenanted with both male and female (Deuteronomy 29:1–11). Women were present in the public reading of the Torah (Deuteronomy 31:9–13; Nehemiah 8:1–3). They served at the tent of meeting (Exodus 38:8; 1 Samuel 2:22) and offered sacrifices (Leviticus 12:1–8; 1 Samuel 2:19). They sometimes performed more prominent roles than their husbands in God's redemptive acts (Judges 13:1–23).[3]

Women as Leaders in the Hebrew Community

Despite the fact that women assumed a lower status than men and were subordinate to their husbands, some women rose to prominent positions in leadership.

Prophetesses

A prophet is a person through whom God speaks. The Hebrew word for prophet is *nabi*. Its feminine form *nebiah* was used to refer to four specific women in the Hebrew Bible.[4] These women included Huldah (2 Kings 22:14); Deborah (Judges 4:4); Miriam (Exodus 15:20) and the nameless woman (Isaiah 8:3). France contended that these women performed prophetic roles rather than holding any formal office.[5] However, some of these women performed well-established and lasting roles.

Miriam

The prophetess Miriam performed a significant role in the purposes of God. She was the sister of Moses and Aaron with whom she shared the leadership of Israel. Micah regarded her leadership as being on par with those of her brothers (Micah 6:3–4). Miriam performed the role of prophetess following Israel's escape from Egyptian bondage when, with a tambourine in hand, she led the Israelite women into a song of dance and praise to God for their newly found freedom. France saw Miriam as holding a subordinate place alongside Moses and Aaron.[6] Swidler noted the discrepancy in the story of Miriam's rebuke when only she was punished with leprosy even though both she and Aaron had criticized Moses for marrying a foreigner, the Cushite woman, and had challenged Moses's sole leadership. Swidler was not sure whether this rebuke was meant to downgrade Miriam in order to elevate Moses and Aaron.[7] Nevertheless, Miriam's prominence in Israelite history was unquestionable as God had confirmed her leadership (Micah 6:4). Her name was recorded in the Israelite genealogy (Numbers 26:59; 1 Chronicles 6:3), and her death was also recorded in the Bible (Numbers 20:1).

Deborah

Deborah was also referred to as a prophetess although she is best remembered for her role as one of Israel's judges. Judges ruled Israel from the time of Moses to the rise of the monarchy (Acts 13:20–21). Deborah was also a military and spiritual leader (Judges 4:4). She functioned as the highest leader in Israel, and she was able to exercise authority over men although she was married (Judges 4:4). She assumed her position of leadership gradually and was initially known to mediate and settle public disputes with God's wisdom among the Israelites who passed through the highlands of Ephraim between Ramah and Bethel.

As a judge, she was a special instrument for dispensing God's justice. She carried out her responsibilities in public view like the other judges by exercising her office in the hill country near to Bethel (Judges 4:5). Bethel was a strategic location that was associated with both religious practices and the prophetic community (1 Samuel 7:16; 2 Kings 2:3, 17:28; Amos 7:10–13). As a part of the prophetic community, she announced God's command to Barak whom she called and ordered to mobilize his troops for war. He responded by encouraging Deborah to accompany him to battle against the superior Canaanites. Thus Deborah assumed military responsibilities. She gave the command to attack after she had directed plans for the military expedition and cleared the way for the soldiers to combat the enemy, thus fulfilling her political role. After Sisera's army was defeated, she served as a spiritual leader when she and Barak joined together as the chief persons to praise God by singing a song of victory. The Song of Deborah (Judges 5:1–31) is perhaps the oldest Hebrew literary composition.[8] Together, Deborah and Barak sang this song as equals. As a woman, Deborah was not expected to submit to the male leadership of Barak.

In her capacity of judge and prophetess, Deborah's calling by God to execute these offices was secure. Despite the restrictions placed on women through Judaic laws and traditions and a preponderance of male judges, the entire Hebrew society accepted her leadership. She displayed tenacity, skill, and wisdom in executing her offices. She was a living testimony and wake-up call to women who struggle to free themselves from the shackles of tradition that weigh heavily upon their leadership in ministry.

Huldah

Huldah was perhaps the most well-known prophetess in the history of Israel (2 Kings 22:14–20). King Josiah singled her out from the male prophets and sought her wise counsel regarding the discovery of the Book of Law in the temple. He sent a delegation of five of his highest court officials, including Hilkiah the High Priest, to consult with Huldah who was believed to be a teacher.

After evaluating the documents, she declared words of judgment on the people's idolatry, resulting in King Josiah leading his people in an act of covenant renewal. This act was, perhaps, the greatest revival in the history of Israel.

Unnamed Woman Prophet

There is also fleeting mention made of the woman prophet in Isaiah 8:13. She bore a child whose name was related to the prophetic mission. She executed her prophetic role anonymously like many other women who assumed prophetic roles and wisely influenced and guided the leaders of their land.[9]

Other Influential Women

There were other influential women many of whom were not considered as prophetesses but who displayed tremendous wisdom, skills, and dexterity. Such women included Judith and Noadiah, who was referred in Nehemiah as a prophetess and who was among Nehemiah's political challengers (Nehemiah 6:14), the unnamed woman and wise woman in 2 Samuel, Esther, and Ruth. Judith acted decisively with wisdom and strong leadership skills to save her people. Her upright life enhanced her leadership (Judith 8:1ff.).

The unnamed woman in 2 Samuel 20:11–22 saved a city from being destroyed because of her wisdom and leadership. There was another wise woman in 2 Samuel 14:2–20 who acted as an intermediary in the return of David's son Absalom from exile.

Esther saved her people, the entire Jewish nation, from extinction by employing initiative, bravery, cunning, and brilliant strategy as a queen to restore the threatened rights of this nation. She risked everything to win her case and secured for her cousin Mordecai the position of Haman, the oppressor in King Ahasuerus's palace (Esther 2:10). As a result of her intervention, the decree against the Jews was rescinded (Esther 8:11–12).

Ruth, the daughter-in-law of Naomi, was praised for her virtuous and upright living. She displayed a quiet and firm leadership in her community (Ruth 3:11).[10] She was regarded as a virtuous woman in her community and showed more kindness to her husband in death than in life. She stuck by her mother-in-law, Naomi's side, after their husbands died.

Hebrew Queens

There were two known Hebrew queens in Judah, Athaliah (842–837) and Salome Alexandra (78–69). After she had put to death all but one of her grandsons who were heirs to the throne, Athaliah became queen and reigned for seven years. She devoted her life to serving Baal and the goddess Asherah. She was regarded as a usurper and was overthrown and assassinated by orders of the Yahwist high priest, Jehoiada. All the people of the land rejoiced at her overthrow (2 Kings 11:1–20).

Salome Alexandra ascended the throne after her husband's death and in fulfillment of his death wish. She reigned for about nine years until her death. She was referred to as Good Queen Alexandra because of the peace and serenity Judah enjoyed during her reign. Judah enjoyed much prosperity and fertility of the soil. Salome Alexandra is believed to have been the last really independent Jewish ruler of the Holy Land until 1948.[11]

Women Leaders in the New Testament

The leadership roles of women in the Old Testament had a tremendous impact on and served as the basis for women leaders of ministry in the New Testament. These leadership roles were performed by such women as Miriam, Deborah, and the other influential women aforementioned. Contrary to the stigma and restrictions that were placed on the status of women in the Hebrew society, the status of women in New Testament times dramatically improved. Their status began to improve with Jesus Christ's attitude toward women that contradicted the attitudes of His contemporaries. He broke Jewish tradition by having women as disciples and traveling companions (Mark 15:40–41; Luke 8:1–3). He taught a woman and defended her choice to learn (Luke 10:38–42). Women were the last to remain at the cross and the first to appear at the tomb. Following His resurrection, Jesus Christ appeared to women first and instructed them to spread the good news to the other disciples (Matthew 28:7).

In addressing the role women played in New Testament history, Hamilton and Hamilton said that the social structure at that time did not permit women to be leaders in the new movement. Although women played a prominent role in the early church, associated with the Apostles, and participated in heading the church movement, the twelve Apostles chosen by Jesus Christ were all men and the early church grew wholly directed by males.[12] Possibly, Jesus Christ might have affirmed male headship and authority when He chose those twelve men to lead the community and recommissioned eleven of these men after His resurrection to continue leading His community. These men were the special companions of Jesus Christ whom He provided with special teaching,[13] thus confirming that Jesus Christ did not abrogate all sexual, social, or creation order distinctions under the Old Covenant even though He deviated from the Jewish tradition. He did not reject the patriarchal framework outright.

Raming believed that when Jesus Christ dealt with women as individuals, His attitude toward them was free from any kind of discrimination. This author argued that even though Jesus Christ had officially appointed only men as apostles and sent them forth, it was not necessarily a deliberate act of Jesus to restrict this office to men only as the Vatican Declaration on the question of the admission of women to the priesthood concluded (v. 1, 1976). By conforming to the existing sociological structures inclusive of the ministry, a public service that was an exclusively male preserve in the Jewish context, Jesus Christ did not necessarily endorse it.[14]

Women Leaders in the Apostolic Church

MacArthur believed that women in the New Testament times did not serve as leaders and that there was no record of women apostles, pastors, teachers, evangelists, or elders. He stated that although women are spiritually equal with men, they are not to function in the same role as men.[15]

The author believes that there are many examples of women who performed bona fide leadership roles in the early church. Although the social structure in apostolic times made it extremely difficult for women to assume leadership roles in the new community, there were several women leaders who rose to prominence in the early church movement. Women were not only full members of the church community, but in the initial phase of the church, they were crucial workers in the spread and administration of Christianity.[16] Some middle-class women were among the first converts. Some of these women were hostesses of house fellowships and served in leadership positions in the life of local churches in the absence of a firm organizational and ministerial hierarchy (Romans 6:1; 1 Corinthians 16:19; Acts 16:14).[17]

Lydia was the first female convert in Europe. She performed a prominent leadership role in ministry when she opened her home for the purpose of a house church (Acts 16:40). Her house church was one of the many house churches, which sprung up everywhere in the Roman Empire under the leadership of women. She was considered the head of her household, which was a deviation from the norm, as women in those days were not usually considered heads of households even after their husbands died. She and her entire household were converted to Christianity. She was a leading member of the church at Philippi and provided hospitality to that church (Acts 14:15, 40).

Leadership roles in the church were not only confined to widows like Lydia or to single women but were also open to married women. Priscilla and her husband, Aquilla, were referred to as coworkers of Paul (Romans 16:3). They were refugees from Rome who performed an instrumental role in founding and establishing the churches at Corinth and Ephesus. Their ministry assisted in fostering the growth of the church. Priscilla was believed to be the more noticeable partner who performed the lead role in teaching Apollo who was an eloquent Jewish teacher and was well versed in the Scriptures (Acts: 18). Paul fully endorsed the leadership contribution of Priscilla in the church[18] and indirectly endorsed the wielding of authority by women in the church. It is believed that Paul placed Priscilla's name before Aquilla's name because she was more of a teacher than he was. After Paul left Corinth, Priscilla pastored the church at Corinth and copastored the church at Ephesus with her husband. Priscilla's ministry was not fleeting. She was firmly grounded as a woman leader.

Paul was commissioned to spread the Word of God to the Gentiles, as well as to the Jews who were scattered throughout the Roman Empire. Women evangelists were among his coworkers who assisted him in propagating and spreading the Gospel. The names of some of these precious and notable women are etched in the annals of the New Testament history. Some passages of scripture that are worthy to note in this regard are Romans 16:1–16 and Philippians 4:2–3.

The following women leaders are worthy of mention: Euodia and Syntyche (Philippians 4:2–3), Nymphia (Colossians 4:15), and Chloe (1 Corinthians 1:11). In Romans 16, Paul sends greetings to approximately twenty-seven of his coworkers, ten of whom were women. Such women included Phoebe, Junia, Persis, Mary, Tryphena, Priscilla, Tryphosa, and Claudia.

Phoebe

Paul recognized Phoebe as his helper and as a servant and helper to the church at Cenchrae where she served in the leadership capacity of deaconess (Romans 16:1–2). She is believed to have been the bearer of Paul's epistle to the Romans who were commanded by Paul to receive her as a leader and to assist her in whatever manner she needed. Paul and other Christians whom she helped loved her. She could not possibly fulfill her duties without speaking in the church.[19]

Junia

Paul greeted Junia in Romans 16:7 as his kindred and coprisoner and as a notable apostle who has been in Christ before him. In some modern translations an *s* is placed at the end of *Junia* as the translators were unsure about a woman being an apostle. Some translators even claim that Andronicus was Junia's husband and that it was he who was accredited with being an apostle and his wife sharing this accreditation with him. This skepticism did not arise until the Middle Ages. However, Chrystostom was quite sure of Junia's gender, and he remarked, "Oh, how great is the devotion of this woman, that she should be even counted worthy of the appellation of apostle!"[20]

The meaning of *apostle* is "one sent forth." In the New Testament times, apostleship was a missionary calling to which vocation some people devoted themselves. They labored with the help of God's Spirit toward the conversion of both Jews and Gentiles.[21] Being an apostle engendered great respect and significant responsibility within the missionary church.[22]

Euodia and Syntyche

Euodia and Syntyche are described as having struggled with Paul and other fellow workers in the Gospel (Philippians 4:2–3). They struggled with Paul alongside such males as Clement, and even though Paul did not describe them by official titles, he did not imply that these women only provided material assistance for him and the other men. This reference in the Word suggests that they played a significant role in the leadership of the church and in preaching, teaching, and spreading the Gospel just as their male counterparts. Paul called them by name and implored them to settle their differences. He placed them on par with the men in the promulgation and spreading of the Gospel.[23]

The Other Women

Paul described Mary as having "worked very hard among you" (Romans 16:6), Tryphena and Tryphosa as "workers in the Lord" (v. 12), and Persis as having "worked hard in the Lord" (v. 12), which suggests that each one of these women held recognized roles of ministry within the church.[24]

Women Leaders in the Pastoral Epistles and Post-Pauline Church

As the church's expectations of the imminent return of Christ began to wane, the ordering of the Pauline communities assumed a hardening of its formal structure to reflect the traditional patriarchal institutions of Judaism and Hellenism. The church reverted to applying the principle of subordination in its ordering of the church community. This principle is reflected in the deutero-Pauline Pastoral Epistles dating back to approximately AD 100. These epistles highlighted rules and regulations for office holders. The ordering of the church community resulted in institutionalization and consolidation of the official hierarchy.[25] However, some forms of service for women in the ministry were still noticeable, such as the "Elect Lady" (2 John 1), the Order of Widows (1 Timothy 5:3–16), and the Office of Deaconesses (1 Timothy 3:11)

The Elect Lady

This term used in 2 John 1 more recently became associated with a female overseer who was similar to a bishop although some people believed that the term referred to a local congregation whose members John referred to as children. The Elect Lady is regarded as having functioned in a pastoral capacity as women such as Lydia (Acts 16:40), Chloe (1 Corinthians 1:11), and Nympha (Colossians 4:15).

Women Presbyters

In 1 Timothy, there are two passages that refer to male presbyters. These are 1 Timothy 4:14 and 1 Timothy 5:17–19. Mention is made of female presbyters in 1 Timothy 5:1–2. The male form *presbytero* means "older man," and the female form *presbyteras* means "older woman." Schmidt felt that the more accurate translation in both 1 Timothy 5:1–2 and 1 Timothy 5:17–19 should be "male presbyter" and "female presbyter."

In another passage of scripture, 1 Timothy 4:14, young Timothy was ordained by the presbytery. Schmidt questioned whether female presbyters were among those who laid hands on Timothy. He noted that the Council of Laodicea (c. 381) ruled that no more women presbyters could be appointed and barred women from "approaching the altar" because presbyters performed liturgical functions.[26]

The Order of Widows

The Order of Widows was one of the earliest Christian offices that were developed for women. It was an independent form of female presbytery that had strict bearing on the separation of the sexes. It was an order that was analogous to that of priests and bishops. Initially, it consisted of Hebrew widows who spent their lives in pursuit of holiness and were connected to Jesus Christ as the Messiah. Anna, the prophetess, was a widow who was connected to Jesus Christ as Messiah. Later on, many widows followed Jesus Christ. It appears that many of the women who ministered to Jesus Christ were widows (Luke 8:1–3; Mark 15:40–41) who searched for holiness.

After the time of Jesus Christ, the Apostle Peter recognized them by setting them specifically apart from other Christian saints and awarding them prominence in the church. In Acts 6:1–2, 9, and 39, "aged widows" were simply to be taken care of by the faith community. Subsequently, these widows had formed an order as mentioned in Acts 9:36, 39–41, where one Tabitha, a disciple, had a group of widows who rallied around her. Also, 1 Timothy 5:3–10 explains how widows in the faith community were to be treated.

The Pauline age requirement for widows was sixty years. Widows were placed in a special category in the church community. To qualify for this category, they had to be at least sixty years old, married once, practiced hospitality, washed the feet of the saints, and were given to good works. In Titus 2:3–4, they were not to exhibit slanderous drunken habits and were to teach young women to love their husbands and children. They were entrusted with the pastoral care of women in their homes and with performing charitable works. They led lives of asceticism at home and devoted themselves to the service of prayer. They were forbidden to perform religious instructions to anyone and to administer the sacraments initially.[27]

However, between the end of the first century and the beginning of the second century, a group of younger women emerged as part of the Order of Widows. Some of these women were unmarried and were under twenty years of age when they joined the order. They were called virginal widows.

Around AD 155, Polycarp, a disciple of Ignatius of Antioch, wrote that the Christian teachings taught by the Apostles were to be passed on to the Order of Widows (Polycarp, Letter to the Philippians IV.3). In the third century, it was believed that widows administered "extreme unction" to dying men. The fifth-century *Statuta ecclesiae antiqua* from South France confirmed that widows were taught in order to instruct women.

The Order of Widows apparently reached its peak around the fifth century as outlined in a Syrian document, the *Testamentum Domini Nostri Jesu Christi*. Widows who had attained the highest status were called pastoral widows or the widows who sit in front. This document mentioned the ordination of widows who were instructed to receive communion with the rest of the clergy, after the deacons and before the readers and subdeacons. Once these widows were ordained, they performed a variety of pastoral duties such as instructing women who went astray, supervising the deaconesses, visiting sick women, and anointing women for baptism.[28]

Women Deacons

The female deaconate was instituted by the Syrian *Didascalia* to serve as a passive tool of the bishop, with a fixed place in the ecclesiastical hierarchy.[29] The deaconate was an ordained office in which both men and women served. It was established in the lifetime of Paul (AD 63). Deaconesses were known in the church since apostolic times. Like the Order of Widows, they remained a distinct ministry within the ordained ministry. When Paul wrote his first epistle to Timothy, both male and female deacons were expected to have parallel qualities (1 Timothy 3:8–11). Although the Greek word *gynaikas*, meaning woman, is used in translating "women deacons" (v. 11), most scholars and Greek fathers like John Chrysostom, Theodore of Mopsuestia, and

Theodoret of Cyrrhus agreed that the necessary characteristics for bishops, deacons, and women deacons are listed in 1 Timothy.[30]

In the third century, the distinct roles of widows and deacons were clearly spelled out, and specific conditions for their ordination were given. With the passage of time, some functions performed by the widows were transferred to the deaconesses, for example, some subordinate duties associated with baptism, such as the anointing of the body, for reasons of decency. However, since the office of deaconess was established by the Syrian *Didascalia*, which gave women a distinct order of ministry "side by side with the bishops, deacons, and priests," there was no clear record regarding the responsibilities of deaconesses. There were records of the decisions taken by a number of councils about what deaconesses were no longer permitted to do. These prohibitions varied from place to place, and as a result, some deaconesses continued to perform services that they might have been prohibited from doing for a while because these services were necessary. Among the councils that made decisions about deaconesses are the Council of Chalcedon (451), which allowed deaconesses on probation to be consecrated at age forty; the Synod of Orange (441), which forbade the ordination of women; and the second Council of Orleans (533), which spoke of deaconesses (presumably ordained) in Gaul and forbade women to pronounce the diaconal benediction because of the "weakness" of their sex.[31]

The development of the office of deaconess reached its peak of development approximately one hundred years later with the *Apostolic Constitutions* believed to have been written in the fourth century and later officially confirmed in the Council of Constantinople (680), which contained a collection of legal and liturgical material. This was a very confusing document, which stated that bishops should anoint only the heads of women and that the deacons should anoint the rest. The deaconess was not to serve at the altar, teach, or baptize. It showed the order of precedence as bishops, presbyters, deacons and deaconesses, and widows. It presented the ordination of a deacon and deaconess as being the same, except that the deacons might aspire to be appointed eventually to higher offices in the church "if they served faithfully and well," and the deaconesses who performed likewise received the prayer of the church for God to grant them the Holy Spirit to "worthily accomplish the work committed to them."[32] Although the deaconess held a place in the official ordering of the church through ordination, the offices held by female deacons were clearly distinguished as being subordinate to other offices held by men. Several Gallican synods of the fourth and sixth centuries prohibited the ordination of deaconesses. However, it must be noted that in the Byzantine part of the church, deaconesses flourished until the eighth and ninth centuries, whereas the Latin-speaking regions such as Italy, North Africa, Brittany, and Gaul had always strongly opposed woman deacons.³³

The Decline of Deaconesses

The decline of this order was aided and abetted by the decline of the Roman Empire. Two reasons were given for its decline. One of these reasons was the woman's "ritual uncleanness" due to her monthly periods. The other reason was the decline in the baptism of adults, which decreased the need for help by women deacons. The Council of Orange (AD 441) Canon 26 forbade anyone to ordain deaconesses anymore. The Council of Epaon (AD 517) Canon 21 abrogated completely the consecration of widows who were called deaconesses in the entire kingdom. The Council of Orleans 11 (AD 533) stipulated that because of the weakness of their sex, women deacons could no longer be given the blessing. By the twelfth century, the order of deaconess had almost totally disappeared from the church. By the Middle Ages, only a few people, perhaps, knew the significance of this order to the early church.³⁴

It must finally be emphasized that, unlike the patriarchal agrarian culture that defined women as being unworthy to be educated and barred them socially and spiritually from executing equal status with men in society, Jesus Christ's attitude toward women transcended some of the traditional norms, rules, and taboos. The Apostolic era ushered into the church a pattern in the ministry of women that was more prominent and dominant and which paved the way in different capacities for women to perform ongoing leadership roles in the propagation of the Gospel and in the establishment of the church.

---

1. Stanley J. Grenz with Denise Muir Kjesbo, *Women in the Church: A Biblical Theology of Women in Ministry* (Downers Grove, Illinois: InterVarsity Press, 1995), 65.
2. Ibid., 66, from Pamela J. Scalese, "Women in Ministry: Reclaiming Our Old Testament Heritage," *Review and Expositor* 83: no.1 (Winter 1986): 8–9.
3. Ibid., 65–66.
4. Leonard Swidler, *Biblical Affirmations of Woman* (Philadelphia: The Westminster Press, 1979), 85.
5. R. T. France, *Women in the Church's Ministry: A Test Case for Biblical Interpretation* (Grand Rapids, Michigan: William B. Eerdmans Publishing Company, 1995), 75.

6. Ibid.
7. Swidler, op. cit., 86.
8. Grenz with Kjesbo, op. cit., 66–68.
9. Elsa Tamez, ed., *Through Her Eyes: Women's Theology from Latin America* (Maryknoll, New York 10545: Orbis Books, 1989), 122.
10. Ibid., 122–125.
11. Swidler, op. cit., 89–90.
12. Kenneth and Alice Hamilton, *To Be a Man, to Be a Woman* (Nashville and New York: Abingdon Press, 1972), 151.
13. Ben Witherington III, *Women and the Genesis of Christianity* (Great Britain: Cambridge University Press, 1990), 111.
14. Virgil Elizondo and Norbert Greinacher, eds., *Women in a Men's Church* (New York: The Seabury Press, 1980), cited from Ida Ramming, "From the freedom of the Gospel to the Petrified 'Men's Church': The Rise and Development of Male Domination in the Church," 5.
15. John MacArthur, *God's Higher Calling for Women: 1 Timothy 2:9–15* (Chicago: Moody Press, 1987), 28–29.
16. Swidler, op. cit., 294.
17. Elizondo and Greinacher, op. cit., 6.
18. France, op. cit., 80–81.
19. Betty Miller, "What Does the Bible Say about Women in Ministry" [Online] Available www.bible.com, 4.
20. John Temple Bristow, *What Paul Really Said about Women: An Apostle's Liberating Views on Equality in Marriage, Leadership, and Love* (San Francisco: Harper, 1991), 57, from Chrysostom, trans. *Nicene and Post Nicene Fathers* (Grand Rapids, Michigan: Eerdmans, 1956), 11:555.
21. Dorothy Pape, *In Search of God's Ideal Woman: A Personal Examination of the New Testament* (Downers Grove, Illinois 60515: InterVarsity Press, 1976), 217, from L. C. Lambert, "Apostles," *International Standard Bible Encyclopedia*: Howard severance Co., 1915.
22. France, op. cit., 87.
23. Alvin John Schmidt, *Veiled and Silenced: How Culture Shaped sexist Theology* (Macon, Georgia 31207: Mercer University Press, 1989), 205.
24. France, op. cit., 85.
25. Elizondo and Greinacher, eds., op. cit., 7.
26. Schmidt, op. cit., 206–207.
27. The History of Women Deacons [Online] Available www.womenpriests.org, 1–2.
28. Swidler, op. cit., 304–308.
29. Elozondo and Greinacher, eds., op. cit., 8.
30. Swidler, op. cit., 309.
31. Elsie Thomas Culver, *Women in the World of Religion* (Garden City, New York: Doubleday & Company, Inc., 1967), 71.
32. Ibid., 72.
33. Elizondo and Greinacher, eds., op. cit., 9.
34. Swidler, op. cit., 314–315.

Chapter Four:
The Question of Ordination

Because of the long history of disagreements and controversy within the church, the issue of the ordination of women to the priesthood has drawn various positions and debates in several denominations, with people changing positions over the centuries. The issue about women not holding authority in the church has persisted while the paradigm of being in favor of or of not being in favor of ordination shifts back and forth. Some people may be willing to change positions in favor of ordination for women, while traditionalists may choose to oppose ordination on the basis that the New Testament upholds general principles of male authority. However, the ordination of women to leadership positions within the ecclesiastic hierarchy has been present in the history of the church dating back to the apostolic era when both deacons and widows were ordained. Present-day ordination of women is merely a resurgence of what existed in the early history of the church.

The Meaning and Purpose of Ordination

Ordination has been a practiced rite for centuries. It is the act by which the community recognizes and confirms the presence of the Holy Spirit's call and endowment on an individual.[1] It is the act by which the community sets apart gifted persons for the effective working of the whole community, toward the completion of their common purpose.[2]

Ordination, which means the laying on of hands, has been present in the church since the apostolic era and was formalized in the third and fourth centuries when it was observed by ritualistic ceremonies for both male and female. From its inception, ordination in the apostolic church afforded women the opportunity to exercise equal rights and privileges and to perform similar tasks like men.

Liefield noted that the New Testament church did not ordain people to positions of authority but designated them to ministries of service. For example, the laying on of hands in 1 Timothy 4:14 and 2 Timothy 1:6 was done in connection with the bestowal of a spiritual gift and not with the conferring of authority or rank. There was no uniform use of the laying on of hands in the scripture, neither was ordination used as a standard for elevating people to a superior rank or authority.

The laying on of hands was done differently in various situations. There are several passages of scripture in the New Testament that deal with this phenomenon. In Acts 6:1–6, hands were laid on seven men who were appointed to attend to the needs of the widows. Acts 9:17 stated the Ananias laid hands on Saul that his sight might be restored and that he might be filled with the Holy Ghost. In Acts 8:17, Peter and John laid hands on converts in Samaria, and they received the Holy Ghost. Paul laid hands on disciples at Ephesus, and they received the Holy Ghost, spoke with tongues, and prophesied (Acts 19:6). Prophets and teachers at Antioch laid their hands on Barnabas and Saul before dispatching them to do the work to which God had called them (Acts 13:3). In the Old Testament, only one example was cited where authority was conferred on the leader Joshua under the guidance of Eleazar, the Priest. Liefield noted that there were no examples where hands were laid on people for the purpose of a ministry of teaching or preaching.

Currently, most evangelical churches practice ordination as the means of appointing people whom God has chosen for the ministry. It is not used to confirm priesthood or a superior rank, exclusive right to exercise certain sacramental rights or governing authority over the church.[3] It is used to confer the Holy Spirit and to commission people for service. If ordination serves these purposes, there is no legitimate reason to support the barring of women from being ordained.

The Ordained Office in the Church

Ordination is acknowledged by almost all traditions as the process whereby leaders are set apart for service within the community of faith. It has been a topic of debate among scholars and theologians with regard to its relevance and validity in ministry. Throughout the history of Christianity, the practice of setting people apart for certain ministries has been a central theme of the church. This rite was derived from both ancient Israel and New Testament times. Today, ordination remains a vital importance for people who are entering pastoral ministry as the need arises for such persons to be set apart for leadership within the church community.

The act of laying on of hands, which is significantly linked with ordination, was practiced in Old and New Testament times. In Numbers 27:18–23, Moses laid hands on Joshua in the presence of Eleazar and the congregation of Israel and charged him to oversee the congregation of Israel. Joshua was endowed with authority and leadership responsibility. Similarly, persons were anointed with oil to assume one of the three offices of prophet, priest, or king. In fact, H. E. Dana confirmed the public nature of this ceremony from studying New Testament texts related to laying on of hands. He described ordination as a "public and formal act employed for the setting apart of people who are called by God to tasks of leadership." He believed that the ceremony of ordination was initiated in apostolic times.[4]

In the New Testament times, Christian ordination was influenced by the appointing of the twelve disciples by Jesus Christ to perform a special function in His ministry. Although the scriptures do not confirm that Jesus Christ laid hands upon those disciples, He set them apart for ministry and, before His departure, recommissioned them to perform leadership roles in the founding of the church. Following the example set by Jesus Christ, the New Testament recorded several incidents of the laying on of hands, for example, 1 Timothy 4:14, where young Timothy was exhorted not to neglect the gift that he was endowed with. His call was publicly confirmed by the laying on of hands by the presbytery. Paul has previously confirmed a divine calling that was pronounced on Timothy's life in previous prophecies on Timothy (1 Timothy 1:18).

Ordination—The Ordained of Today

The rite of ordination continues to be practiced today in Christian communities. It includes the laying on of hands, which is a part of the ceremony and, in the context of the church, is tightly interwoven with the concepts of priesthood of believers and the priesthood of gifted persons. The New Testament presents a new priesthood that is in contrast to the Old Testament male priesthood, which permitted only men to serve in the priesthood. Emphasis is now placed on the priesthood of believers, that is, the church as a whole. It encompasses the priesthood and not solely the ordained office. Grenz and Kjesbo referred to the church as a fellowship of believer priests. Because of the sacrificial work of Jesus Christ as High Priest, all believers can now approach God's throne of mercy with boldness and receive mercy (Hebrews 4:15–16). Believers are invited, in Hebrews 10:19–22, to enter the most Holy Place where only High Priests in Old Testament times had the prerogative to enter. In 1 Peter 2:5 and 9, believers are presented as a holy priesthood offering up spiritual sacrifices, acceptable to God by Jesus Christ, and as a chosen generation, a royal priesthood, a holy nation, and a peculiar people. All believers are endowed with this status, both males and females. No longer is the clergy viewed as mediator between God and the people.[5]

Priesthood, in general terms, encompasses the entire body of Christ. The very foundation of the ordained office emerges from the ministry of the entire fellowship of believers, and its foundation lies within the entire church. The pastorate is viewed as an extension of the universal ministry of Christ's body that is best fulfilled by both men and women in partnership with one another.[6]

Spiritual Gifts and the Ordained Office

All believers are now participants in the ministry of the entire fellowship of believers and, as such, are endowed with specific gifts to contribute to the universal ministry of the church. The risen Jesus Christ, who gives spiritual gifts, and the Holy Spirit, who carries out the instructions of Jesus Christ through His sovereign will, bestow spiritual gifts on all believers (Ephesians 4:7–11; 1 Corinthians 12:7–11). These spiritual gifts are given to the body of Christ for the common good of the entire body (1 Corinthians 12:7) and in the use of the fivefold ministry—apostle, prophet, evangelist, pastor, and teacher—the perfecting of the saints, the work of the ministry, and the edifying of the body of Christ (Ephesians 4:11, 12).

The ordained ministry is directly linked with the fivefold ministry, with its pastoral leadership component. The Holy Spirit wills both male and female into this ministry regardless of their race, gender, or social status to perform various leadership functions in the church. For persons who are called to pastoral leadership, ordination serves to commission them into special ministries for the mission of the church, their chief responsibility being "to assemble and build up the church by proclaiming and teaching the Word of God by celebrating the sacraments and by guiding the life of the community in its worship, its mission, and its caring ministry."[7] These pastoral leaders are placed as overseers over the community.

If ordination to pastoral leadership is embedded in the Holy Spirit's universal endowment of all to the task, if the Holy Spirit wills some people to pastoral leadership within the universal ministry, if ordination does not necessitate one person lording it over other Christians but facilitates that person focusing on serving in a special ministry on behalf of the entire church,[8] then ordination of women to (pastoral) leadership in ministry must be sanctioned by the Holy Spirit in the context of the entire community of faith. If the Holy Spirit has already (called and) endowed certain women to serve in the area of leadership, He has also placed the responsibility on the community to recognize, confirm, and sanction these women's capacity and personal desire to serve as leaders. To resist or to downplay such women as leaders is to defy the Holy Spirit's final authority and omniscience and to focus on upholding certain traditions and structural constraints in the church. Such traditions and structural constraints are most likely outdated and no longer serve any purpose in the growth of the body of Christ. There are no plausible reasons why women who are a part of the faith community and of the universal priesthood of believers should be denied ordination since they are called by the Holy Spirit to minister.

Ordination of Women and New Testament Principles

When examining the ordination of women in the context of the New Testament, France noted that the first-century society was strongly male dominated, which in turn was reflected in the relationship between male and female as is evident in the New Testament. However, he contended that a male-dominated society could not be considered as an inevitable part of the divine purpose. The general principle of male authority in the New Testament is upheld by some people as the rationale for denying women ordination to the priesthood. France refuted this argument for two reasons. Firstly, he argued that what God intended for society and what He intended for the church are not necessarily the same. The church is expected not to imitate the norms and values of the secular society but to be a "peculiar" people who are set apart from the world, though in the world, and who should be exercising the God-given ideals of human relationships. The Bible does not declare that male authority should be a monopoly within the church. This principle cannot be considered the ideal of human relationship in the priesthood of believers. Secondly, France argued that the New Testament principle of male leadership and female submission is applicable to the marriage relationship and not to the entire structure of society. He supported this principle as being ideal for the marriage relationship but not for human life in general.[9]

His line of argument justifies the right for women outside the marriage relationship to be ordained to the ministry. However, it must be recognized that within the marriage relationship, the wives may be chosen by the Holy Spirit to assume leadership positions. Then a more complex issue arises as to whether these women should be ordained to these leadership positions and, if they are ordained, what issues may arise for the proponents of male leadership, especially within a local congregation. This view of male leadership holds serious implications for women within and without the context of the marriage relationship. Some people may put forward the argument that, within the marriage relationship, the husband should perform the role of elder in a local congregation to ensure that male leadership is enforced. However, the gifts of the Holy Spirit on people's lives must be recognized as the most crucial determining factor in arriving at the decision to confer the office of elder on husbands who may not necessarily be appropriate for this office. On the other hand, husbands who are capable of serving in this capacity may be instrumental in the organization of local congregations.

France was careful to examine two passages of scripture on which opponents of women ordination have based their argument and which need to be mentioned in order to create some balance in his argument. These passages are 1 Corinthians 14:34–35 and 1 Timothy 2:8–15. He acknowledged that the first passage of scripture is difficult to interpret as it is uncertain whether Paul was referring to a particular type of speaking such as speaking in tongues or interpretation of tongues or whether he was referring to the chattering of women to disturb the worship of the congregation. He believed that Paul might not have been speaking to women in general but to married women who behaved unseemly. He concluded that this passage did not forbid women to perform any speaking roles in the church as Paul's letter to the Corinthians revealed that women prophesied in the congregation.

First Timothy 2:8–15 was written amid the prevailing religious practices in Ephesus, which revolved around the temple of Armetis and its cultic practices. The church that Timothy was placed in charge of might have been adversely affected by these cultic practices. It seemed that within that local congregation, there were some localized currents of teaching and behavior pertaining to women that were problematic and that in this passage of scripture, Paul's concern was about the appropriate role of the wife as related to her husband in the context of worship. This being so, the question arises as to whether this text could be applied to the roles of men and women outside the institution of marriage.[10]

Women Ordination—A Radical Departure from the Traditional Roles

Although the ordination of women may be seen as a radical departure from the traditional roles of women in the church, such as Sunday school teachers, Bloomquist regarded women's ordination as a continuity of the traditional roles of women in the home and in the church. She focused on the nurturing role of women in caring for their families, which the church recognizes and sanctions. She stated that this nurturing service role is similar to the role of the ordained minister. Mostly, women are intended to be religious teachers in the home and in church schools. Mainly, women fill many present-day "caring" or helping vocations such as social work, nursing, and teaching of small children. Bloomquist argued that women more closely represent the model of the ideal Christian life of self-sacrificing love for others. This fact is overlooked in the services that women provide in the church, resulting in women performing countless hours of volunteer church labor and being paid low wages as most church secretaries.[11]

Byrne also commented on the nurturing role of the church in terms of the priesthood. She contended that the presence of women in the priesthood has imaged a God who nurtures and empowers and is both life and love. This image of the priesthood is viewed in terms of being embodied in a priest who nurtures and empowers and is life and love. The challenge of priesthood is the ability to find ways of nurturing, which is in keeping with the insight that Christians are called to adult life in the church. Therefore, the patriarchal pastor should give way to the images of a nurturing presence that places emphasis on human development. Females whose model of engagement is a nurturing one best epitomize this presence.[12]

Some people may argue that the pastoral office should be limited to men because Jesus Christ was a male and the Bible portrays God more as a male than as a female. As a pastoral leader, the male bears the divine image of God to a greater degree than a female. For these people, an ordained minister is the representative of God to the congregation; therefore, a woman is unable to adequately fulfill the pastoral office. However, in the Bible,

God is portrayed by both male and female images, which suggest that He is nonsexual. He alone is God and is first and foremost a Spirit. It is irrelevant therefore to refer to Him as either a male or a female God.

Some people understand the metaphoric analogy of God the "Father" as speaking of a male deity. Grenz and Kjesbo suggested that this paternal metaphor is merely the best image for conveying a dimension of the divine reality that God wants us to understand.[13]

Barton pointed out that the Doctrine of God the Father is an analogy of the providence of God and a sense of God's care for the whole of creation. This analogy does not describe God's gender because God is beyond gender.[14]

Boucher understood the metaphors of God "the Father" and "the Son" as not expressing sexual character in neither the divine nature nor in the Persons. She noted that theologians in the first and second centuries regarded God the Father as the creator and author of all things and God the Son as being like the First Person and being from the Father.[15]

In referring to God, the scriptures also portray metaphors of maternal nurture as in Isaiah 1:2 and Isaiah 49:13–15.

Opposing Views Regarding the Ordination of Women

Views regarding the ordination of women stem from two schools of thought. These schools of thought either support or oppose the ordination of women. People who oppose the ordination of women justify their opposition based on the principle of the submission of women to men and on certain biblical texts that they believe support the exclusion of women from exercising the functions of ordained ministry. They put forward the view that women were involved in ordained ministry in a limited manner and that the twelve disciples that were chosen by Jesus Christ for the inner circle were all males. They subscribe to the view that the leadership principle of man over woman is not only used by Paul in the context of marriage but also in reference to the respective roles of men and women in worship (1 Corinthians 11:3).

Opponents to women's ordination stress the view that women cannot be ordained to the priesthood because of the nature of the priesthood that is of a sacramental nature involving sacramental signs. The priest is regarded as a sign that draws its supernatural effectiveness from ordination. He is required to have a natural resemblance to Christ. Because Jesus Christ was a man, only a male can express His role in the Eucharist sacramentally. Only in a male can the image of Christ be seen.

Opponents to women's ordination also argue that Jesus Christ intended to exclude women from the priesthood because He did not ordain women to be apostles. They claim that the intent and authority of Jesus Christ in excluding women should not be denied. Several views have been put forward to dispute this argument. It could be argued that Jesus Christ did not ordain anyone or that the apostles included a number of persons who were not appointed by Jesus Christ. There were women among the apostles, such as Junia (Romans 16:7). It could also be argued that even though women were not among the apostles of Jesus Christ, He did not intend to exclude them. He might have had a sound reason for not including them.

Amid all speculations, Jesus Christ was fully cognizant of His choice of male apostles. In appointing twelve Jewish males to be His inner circle, Jesus Christ intended the church to be the new Israel, the successor of the twelve tribes. Because of the symbolic conventions of His social milieu, He could not choose women or Gentiles to be included in His inner circle.[16]

Foh identified four categories of improper arguments against the ordination of women. One argument is based on the nature of woman. Women are inferior and cannot become ministers. The second argument involves the nature of God. God is Father, and Jesus Christ His Son was reincarnated as a man. The minister represents God and should be male. Then there is the argument from biblical example. Jesus Christ chose twelve male disciples. The last argument is based on tradition. Throughout the history of the (early) church, women were not ordained as ministers. Foh did not subscribe to the arguments based on biblical example, tradition, experience, the universal priesthood of believers, preaching as being equivalent to prophecy, and women being allowed to prophecy. She did not view the biblical text of Galatians 3:28 as a ground for the ordination of women. She cited the only valid argument against women's ordination as the scriptural prohibition of 1 Timothy 2:12, which bars women from becoming ministers, that is, elders or pastor-teachers because elders teach (1 Timothy 3:2) and rule (1 Timothy 5:17).

On the matter of biblical example, Foh contended that women did not participate equally and fully with men from the beginning of the church as they did not teach the assembly or a miscellaneous group. Were there no house churches in the early history of the church over which some women presided? As house churches sprang up everywhere, it is very likely that women leaders preached the Word of God and taught the members of those churches. Foh noted that although women participated in invaluable activities in the church traditionally, they were not ordained to the ministry. Although experience has shown that there were and are dynamic women preachers, evangelists, pastors, and teachers, Foh argued that the Holy Spirit who wrote the scriptures will not contradict Himself by endowing women with a position He denied them in the Word. However, the author believes that since there are no male or female gifts, similar gifts may be bestowed on both males and females. Foh argued that the universal priesthood of believers argument is not related to the ministry but to our offering of ourselves as spiritual sacrifices to God (Romans 12:1; 1 Peter 2:5) and to our access to God through Christ's blood (Hebrews 10:19–22). Even though both male and female can be regarded as priests in these regards, this status does not qualify people for any church office. She defined the functions of the minister as teaching God's word, administering the sacraments, caring for the congregation, and governing the congregation, including church discipline, thus implying that women are not qualified to perform these functions. She argued that preaching and prophecy are not the same and that although women were allowed to prophecy (1 Corinthians 11:3–16), they were forbidden to teach. She stressed that preaching is a form of teaching, which results from the speaker's preparation and study. Are women incapable of performing these tasks? The Bible is fraught with examples of women who performed these tasks, with signs and wonders following. Some examples of such women are noted in chapters 3 and 5. She interpreted Galatians 3:28 to mean that all believers are equally important in the kingdom of God but that this scripture does not allow people the right to become heads or eyes or ears (1 Corinthians 12:14–30).[17] The Holy Spirit endows people with this right and responsibility. Some very pertinent questions to consider are the following: Is it man who determines who should be called to pastoral ministry? Does the grace of God extend only to men where specific gifts are concerned?

In addressing the question of women priests, Daly made a few observations. She stressed that only women are identified with their sexual functions in the context of the church, which is a deep-rooted prejudice. She further stated that if qualified people are excluded from any ministry because of their sex, there will be no equality of men and women in the church. She also noted that once a significant distinction remains between the hierarchy and laity in the church and if women are denied the option of becoming priests (or pastors), their position among the people of God is radically affirmed. She felt that the ordination of women couldn't be separated from the political emancipation of women. One should not be accepted and the other rejected.[18] She cited Professor Stendahl saying, "If emancipation is right, then there is no valid 'biblical' reason not to ordain women. Ordination cannot be treated as a 'special' problem since there is no such indication that the New Testament sees it as such."[19]

Dr. W. A. Visser 't Hooft, then General Secretary of the World Council of Churches, at one of its conferences, stated that "in this age of emancipation of races, of women, by a natural historic process, Christians have not to argue about rights, but about opportunities for people to make their spiritual contributions. The whole church cannot afford to deprive itself of the gifts God is trying to administer. The reason for the emancipation of women in the church is not the barren fight for the rights of women, but the fruitful discovery of their spiritual gifts, of their full creative contributions."[20]

Positions of Various Denominations on the Question of Ordination of Women

The matter of women's ordination to the preaching ministry has been a topic of debate in the first half of the twentieth century in protestant denominations as well the Anglican, Roman Catholic, and Eastern Orthodox faiths. In the nineteenth century, the Catholic and Calvinistic doctrines of woman's inferior position and intellect were taught from the pulpit. Protestant clergy and the Greek Orthodox faith also upheld these views. However, the first wave of liberal thinking came to light in the Seneca Falls Women's Rights Convention in 1848 in which the Declaration of the Rights of Women was based on the American Declaration of Independence and Bill of Rights. It declared that men and women were born equal and supported the inclusion of women in theological study, teaching, and ministry.[21]

Lucretia Mott, a Quaker minister, ended this convention with a final resolution in which she declared that the speedy success of (women's) cause depended on "the zealous and untiring effort of both men and women for the overthrow of the monopoly of the pulpit and for the securing to women of equal participation with men in various trades, professions and commerce."[22] Lucretia Mott and her counterpart, Esther Moore, and the Grimké sisters, Sarah and Angelina of South Carolina were against slavery and very vocal. Their efforts and increasing power and influence drew fear from the church. For example, the Orthodox Congregational, the largest and most influential ecclesiastical body of Massachusetts, began to protest against the abolitionists for allowing women to speak in public. In 1837, the General Assembly of Massachusetts issued a pastoral letter requesting all churches under their care to close their doors to the abolitionists who permitted women to speak on their platform in public. A woman was viewed as assuming the place and tone of a man as a public reformer, which could not be tolerated. This general assembly voiced the opinion that the appropriate duties and influence of women are spelled out in the New Testament. They regarded a woman as wielding mighty power in her dependence (on man) in the weakness that God has given her. She was to appropriately involve herself in activities that were suitable for the modesty of her sex. Such activities included propagating the cause of religion at home and abroad, in Sabbath schools, and in leading religious inquirers to the pastors for instruction.[23] To be a public reformer, a woman was considered to wield "manly" power, which was totally out of keeping with what was condoned as acceptable behavior for a woman.

Despite this voice of dissension in the church, a few Protestant churches began to ordain women in the nineteenth century. Among these were the Congregationalists who were not opposed to women on the pulpit although there was a scarcity of facilities for the training of women for the ministry. In addition to the Congregational church, other liberal churches such as the Unitarians, Evangelical and Pentecostal Revivalists in which institutional office gave way to the gifts of the Holy Spirit, permitted women to occupy pulpit ministries. More recently, some evangelical denominations such as the Evangelical Lutheran Church in America, the United Church of Christ, the American Baptist Churches, the Presbyterian Church USA, the Christian Church, and the United Methodist Church have been ordaining women. It must be noted that most churches that ordain women hold a more liberal interpretation of the Bible. Fundamentalist churches, as well as the Roman Catholic and Orthodox churches continue to reject the ordination of women.[24]

In 1853, the first woman, Antoinette Brown, was ordained to the congregational ministry. Luther Lee, an evangelical preacher, led the ordination service. He preached his sermon from Galatians 3:28 and Acts 2:17–18. He believed that the preaching office and the prophetic office are the same, that the gift of prophecy is given to both man and woman, and that there was no excuse for excluding women from the ordained ministry.[25] Antoinette Brown obtained a theological degree at Oberlin.

The theological scene in the United States remained a heated battleground in the nineteenth century as obstacles to women ministers surged. Amid much objection, Olympia Brown, who had studied at St. Lawrence College, was ordained in 1864. On July 18, 1878, a series of resolutions supporting women's equality and religious rights with men was passed in Rochester, New York. Immediately following the passing of these resolutions, Rev. R. A. Strong, DD, President of the Rochester Theological (Baptist) Seminary, was so enraged by their endorsement that he preached a sermon opposing them. In essence, he put forward several arguments to support a woman's subordination in office to a man and in the order of creation. This sermon influenced the United Presbyterian Assembly to pass a resolution in 1878, finding no insufficient justification in scripture to ordain women as deacons.[26] This assembly specified that women would be allowed to serve in the capacity of assistants to deacons. Strong's sentiments were endorsed by other preachers such as Rev. Knox Little of England, who, in the fall of 1880, preached a sermon entitled "Sermon to Women" in the church of St. Clemens, in Philadelphia, USA. The *Times* of that day reported the main features of that sermon as being "a representation of a woman's inferior intellect; her duty of unqualified obedience to her husband, however evil his life; the sinfulness of divorce; and the blessedness of a large family of children."[27] It is regrettable that even in the twenty-first century there are still many theologians, denominations, and Christians who endorse this position. Because of such proponents, the issue of women leaders in ministry and more specifically the ordination of women leaders will continue to be a heated matter for debate.

History reveals that some denominations such at the Congregationalists, now the United Church of Christ, were accepting the ordination of women in the United States of America. In New England, for example, many women of distinction served in several parishes. However, it was not until the 1950s to 1970s that major Protestant denominations began to ordain women and a significant number of women began to attend seminaries and to be ordained for ministry.[28]

With the increased ratio of church denominations in the USA in the middle of the nineteenth century such as the Anglican, Lutheran, Presbyterian, and Roman Catholic Churches came more structure and the emergence of different forms of hierarchy. Despite this fact, however, women played a very significant leadership role in pioneering churches as there was a dearth of trained male ministers to serve as resident pastors.

The Methodist Church

The Wesleyan Methodist Church ordained its first woman in the early 1860s and the Methodist Episcopal in 1869. Ms. Frances Willard, who founded the World Women's Christian Temperance Union, served awhile as D. L. Moody's assistant. In 1880, she wrote "Women in the Pulpit," defending the ministry of women.[29] However, when the first woman, Anna Snowden, under the assumed surname of Oliver, enrolled in the school of theology at Boston University, the Methodist Church created an uproar. Anna Oliver graduated in 1876 amid much controversy and continued to be a Methodist minister until 1893. She had a black evangelist, Amanda Smith, as her assistant.[30] In May 1880, she pled her cause for full installment and ordination before the general conference of the Methodist Episcopal Church.

Another woman of caliber was Ms. Betsy Dow, the first female theological instructor at Newbury Biblical Institute between 1837 and 1838. She continued to teach theology as long as she remained at that school, which subsequently became associated with Boston University School of Theology, a renowned Methodist theological school in the United States of America.

Initially, the Methodist Church placed women on par with men in ministry. Subsequently, more and more restrictions were placed on women. Although they could be ordained for either a teaching or preaching ministry, problems arose in placing female ministers where married (male) ministers were favored. Married male ministers lived in parsonages with their families, usually for brief periods of time. Ordained women could not be members of the annual conferences where appointments to pulpit ministry were made. As a result, most theologically trained women took to teaching or missionary work.

A significant breakthrough in ordination in the Methodist Church was realized in the 1950s in the United States of America after a 1950 census of women preachers had revealed that 6,777 women in the USA were clergywomen and that 5,791 of them were ordained or licensed. Astonishingly, fewer than 2,900 of the preachers were pastors of local churches, and most of the registered clergywomen were in the smallest churches. Around 10 percent of them were involved in churches that were affiliated with the National Council of Churches. Very few of these female pastors were senior pastors. The majority of female pastors were involved in teaching jobs, religious education, or mission work. The Methodist Church, which had previously ordained women on a restricted basis, granted full clergy rights to women at a general conference in 1956.[31]

The Presbyterian Church

The Presbyterian Church followed the example of the Methodist Church, and in 1956, the United Presbyterian Church ordered the ordination of women to the full ministry of the church. This denomination placed much emphasis on examining the matter of ordination since 1953. The ordination of women pastors was incorporated into the constitution of the general assembly in 1956 to mark the 250th anniversary of the Presbyterian Church. In 1964, the Southern Presbyterian Church ordained its first female pastor, a grandmother.[32]

The Lutheran Church

The objection raised by some Lutherans to the ordination of women in the United States of America is based on the premise that women pastors would have authority over men. This principle seemed unfounded to them. Meanwhile, women priests in Scandinavia have been winning their struggle for ordination sanctioned by the state. Despite some dissension among the bishops, the struggle in Sweden lessened when a proposal was made to deny the appointment of any pastor as a bishop if he refused to ordain a woman. As a result, three women were ordained to the ministry in April 1960. Some Swedish Lutheran pastors raised the idea of boycotting women pastors by arguing that their acceptance could pose a serious threat to the church of Sweden and that of England, which mutually accept each other's priests. When objections were raised in Norway regarding the ordination of the first female pastor, Mrs. Ingrid Bjerkas, a retired male pastor was appointed as her assistant.[33]

The Church of England

In the middle of the nineteenth century, there was dissension among the members of the Church of England concerning the ministry of women, in particular, the female deaconate. Although a woman was ordained as a deacon in 1862, resulting in the emergence of the Anglican Deaconesses Community of St. Andrews, it was not until 1987 that women were admitted to the full order of deacons. By 1992, 1,300 women deacons were ordained.

The mother church, the Church of England, was slow to make progress in ordaining women to the ministry. In November 1984, the matter of the ordination of women was discussed in synod. Although a clear majority voted in favor of ordination, it was not until November 1992 that this vote was ratified by a two-thirds majority of bishops, priests, and laity. Finally, the Church of England had opened its doors to ordaining women as priests.[34]

In Hong Kong, one Florence Li Tim-Oi was ordained as an Anglican priest in 1944. The Episcopal Church in the United States of America irregularly ordained women priests in 1974. In other parts of the world, Anglican Churches such as the church in Canada have ordained women as priests in 1976. That same year, the General Convention of the Episcopal Church regularized the ordination of women to the priesthood. The move to regularize the ordination of women was opposed and still is opposed by an active minority within the church. The Anglican Church in New Zealand began to ordain women in 1977 and in Kenya and Uganda since 1983. However, there are still churches in the Anglican community, one of the three major church bodies, that do not ordain women. The decision of the General Convention in 1976 that resulted in polarization within the Anglican denomination also resulted in an unholy alliance of conservative Catholics and Evangelicals. Although the decision engendered stiff opposition against the ordination of women, this opposition did not verify that women could not be ordained.

The rapid rise of women's ordination was profoundly influenced by the women's movements that had gained a strong voice in the culture at large. Particularly, women's ordination gained momentum in the mainline Protestant denominations in the 1970s when the number of women ordained in some denominations rose to about 60 percent in a few years. Older arguments based on the biblical prohibition of women ministers and on the conservative "tradition" that opposed women's ordination were disregarded and superseded by arguments that were based on notable women in the Bible, such as Deborah and Phoebe, and on Galatians 3:28, which advocates spiritual equality, to justify the claim for more women leaders within the Christian community.[35]

The Orthodox and Roman Catholic Churches

Two other major church bodies, the Greek Orthodox and Roman Catholic Churches, have assumed a strong stance against the ordination of women.

The Greek Orthodox Church holds the belief that the special ordination for the performance and transmission of the sacraments belong to the male sex. The Greek Orthodox churches of the East, just like the Roman Catholic churches, hold fast to the apostolic tradition by remaining faithful to the teachings and practices of the college of the Apostles. They believe that the successors to the apostles must hand down what they received from the apostles and that only men should be ordained to Holy Order. Rev. Fr. Charles E. Irvin remarked that it would be virtually impossible for either the Orthodox Church or the Catholic Church to ordain women, given their history from apostolic times. However, he does acknowledge that the Holy Spirit's intervention can change this tradition of twenty centuries.[36]

In the Catholic Church, the Vatican has put forward the argument against women priests based on church tradition. For example, the 1977 Vatican Declaration on the Ordination of Women claimed that it has been a constant tradition since the time of Jesus Christ and the apostles for women to be excluded from the priesthood. The Vatican regards this exclusion as originating from God's dispensation. It supports the view that the priest who officiates at the Eucharist acts in the person of Christ and, through the natural resemblance mainly through his maleness to Christ, serves as an easily recognizable "sign." The document concluded that women were not called to the priesthood. In 1994, Pope John Paul II, in his Apostolic Letter *Ordinatio sacerdotalis* (Priestly ordination) reaffirmed the traditional Catholic position against women's ordination and stressed that Christ chose twelve men to be apostles. He also stressed that the church did not have the authority to endorse women's ordination.[37]

Luis T. Gutierrez strongly contended that the ordination of women is a prerequisite for Christian unity (Vatican II, Ecumenism, 2). Although the male-only priesthood has been in effect for two thousand years, he regarded it as a "counter-witness to the mysteries of the incarnation and the redemption." The priestly ordination of women must take place for the sake of the kingdom. He saw the necessity for the church to have both mothers and fathers to take care of God's children and supported the ordination of women to the deaconate and of celibate women to the priesthood and the episcopate.[38]

Freewill Baptists

Even before 1800, the Freewill Baptists allowed women to serve as preachers and itinerant evangelists. Under Charles G. Finney, the great revival culminated in the full ordination of women.

The Southern Baptist Convention

Initially, ordained women served in various capacities in this denomination. However, it never formally approved of women assuming pastoral positions. Serious attention was directed to this issue in the Southern Baptist Convention of 1984 when women were discouraged from seeking pastoral leadership positions. In 1987, the Home Mission Board voted in favor of denying financial assistance to any congregation that had a female pastor on staff. Between 1986 and 1992, there was a significant rise in the number of ordained women. However, these women did not serve as senior pastors but in other capacities such as chaplains or Christian educators.

The North American Baptist Conference

This conference came into existence to examine the issue of women in ministry. It endorsed the local congregation as being responsible for ordination with the advice and consent of the regional association. In 1985 and about 1992, two task forces concluded that the ordination of women was appropriate in the North American Baptist Conference churches but that women were not to serve in the capacity of senior pastors.

The Conservative Baptist Association

This association sought advice from the National Coordinating Council regarding ordaining women on the pastoral staff. In turn, the National Coordinating Committee asked a study committee to examine the issue. This committee produced a document that put forward three positions, namely, the egalitarian position, which believed that all ministry positions should be opened to both qualified men and women; the moderate position, which supports the office of elder (senior pastor) to be closed to women; and the complementarian position, which stipulates that women should be restricted from participating in ministries that require them to exercise authority over or teach men. In the final analysis, this association continued to struggle with the issue of the ordination of women. At its annual meeting in Orlando in 1992, a decision was taken to deny admission into the association any church with a female senior pastor. The churches have not been presenting females for ordination.[39]

---

1. Ibid., 196.
2. Ibid., 196, from *Baptism, Eucharist and Ministry*, 30.
3. Bonnidell Clouse and Robert G. Clouse, eds., *Women in Ministry: Four Views* (Downers Grove, Illinois 60515: InterVarsity Press, 1989), in Walter L. Liefield, "A Plural Ministry View: Your Sons and Your Daughters Shall Prophesy," 144–145.
4. Stanley J. Grenz with Denise Muir Kjesbo, *Women in the Church: A Biblical Theology of Women in Ministry* (Downers Grove, Illinois: InterVarsity Press, 1995), 195, from H. E. Dana, "Ordination in the New
5. Ibid., 183.
6. Ibid., 187.
7. Ibid., 197, from *Baptism, Eucharist and Ministry*, Faith and Order Paper III (Geneva: World Council of Churches, 19820, 22.
8. Ibid., 197.
9. R. T. France, *Women in the Church's Ministry: A Test Case for Biblical Interpretation* (Grand Rapids, Michigan: William B. Eerdmans Publishing Company, 1995), 35–37.
10. Ibid., 36–38, 51–61.
11. Clare Benedicks Fischer, Betsy Brenneman, and Anne McGrew Bennett, *Women in a Strange Land: Search for a New Image* (Philadelphia: Fortress Press, 1975), 69–70, cited from Karen L. Bloomquist, "We as Ministers, Amen!"
12. Lavinia Byrne, *Women Before God: Our Own Spirituality* (Mystic, Connecticut: Twenty-Third Publications, 1988), 129–132.
13. Grenz with Kjesbo, op. cit., 144–147.
14. Ibid., 147, cited from Stephen C. Barton, "Impatient for Justice: Five Reasons Why the Church of England Should Ordain Women to the Priesthood," *Theology* 92, no. 749 (September 1989): 404.
15. Ibid., in Madeleine Boucher, "Ecumenical Documents: Authority in Community," *Midstream* 21, no.3 (July 1982): 409.
16. Ursula King, ed., *Women in the World's Religions: Past and Present* (New York: Paragon House, 1987), 145–155, in Harriet E. Baber, "The Ordination of Women, Natural Symbols, and What Even God Cannot Do."

17. Clouse and Clouse, op. cit., 90–94, cited from Susan Foh, "A Male Leadership View: The Head of the Woman Is the Man."
18. Mary Daly, *The Church and the Second Sex* (Boston, Massachusetts 02108: Beacon Press, 1968), 197–198.
19. Ibid., 198, in Krister Stendahl, *The Bible and the Role of Women: A Case Study in Hermeneutics*, trans. by Emilie T. Sander (Philadelphia: Fortress Press, Facet Books, Biblical Series 15, 1966), 39.
20. Elsie Thomas Culver, *Women in the World of Religion* (Garden City, New York: Doubleday & Company Inc., 1967), 212.
21. Rosemary Radford Ruether, *Sexism and God Talk: Toward a Feminist Theology* (Boston: Beacon Press, 1983), 199.
22. Ibid., in "Declaration of Sentiments and Resolutions: Seneca Falls, July 19, 1848," in *Feminism, The Essential Historical Writings*, ed. M. Schneir (New York: Vintage, 1972), 76–82.
23. Matilda Joslyn Gage, *Woman, Church and State* (New York: Arno Press, 1972), 471–472.
24. Ursula King, *Women and Spirituality: Voices of Protest and Promise*, Second Edition (University Park, Pennsylvania: The Pennsylvania State University Press, 1993), 182.
25. Ruether, op. cit., 198–199.
26. Gage, op. cit., 469–477.
27. Ibid., 492.
28. Ruether, op. cit., 199–200.
29. Dorothy R. Pape, *In Search of God's Ideal Woman: A Personal Examination of the New Testament* (Downers Grove, Illinois 60515: InterVarsity Press, 1976), 228.
30. Culver, op. cit., 214–215.
31. Ibid., 216–218.
32. Ibid., 217–218.
33. Ibid., 219–220.
34. Marga Buhrig, *Woman Invisible: A Personal Odyssey in Christian Feminism* (Tunbridge Wells, Kent: Burns & Oates, 1993), 109–110.
35. Elizabeth A. Clark and Herbert Richardson, eds., *Women and Religion*, new revised and expanded edition (San Francisco: Harper, 1996), 163.
36. Rev. Fr. Charles E. Irvin, "The Ordination of Women," *San Francisco Bay Catholic External Report* [Online], available http://www.rc.net/lansing/ st_mary/essays/ordwomen.html.
37. Clark and Richardson, op. cit., 263–264.
38. Luis T. Guttierez, "The Male-Only Priesthood Is Not Revealed Truth" [Online] Available SF Bay Catholic Electronic Magazine, mailed January 4, 1996.
39. Grenz with Kjesbo, op. cit., 27–30.

Chapter Five:
Women Leaders in Contemporary Times

From a historical viewpoint, women have been targeted in the Judeo-Christian tradition for exclusion from leadership roles and from visibility. This situation has existed for several centuries. It has resulted in women being led to assume stereotypical positions such as teachers in Sunday schools, instead of positions in colleges and seminaries like their male counterparts. Amid this oppression, some women succeeded in rising to positions within the church. For example, Catherine of Siena was a dominant figure in the Western Church in the Middle Ages.

Anne Hutchinson (1591–1643) became very influential in Boston in the Puritan era. She was extremely skillful exegetically and homiletically and versed in spiritual truths, which brought her great success as a formidable leader in the Christian community. Her followers included both males and females. Zealous New England ministers noted her successes. She was accused of heresy and banished from Massachusetts, Bay Colony, in 1638.

Margaret Fell (1614–1702), the mother of Quakerism, used her home to hold meetings and to shelter the persecuted Quakers. Although imprisoned for four years for her religious activities, she became an itinerant preacher in jails and in remote farms and villages. She excelled in wisdom and was able to write many tracts and letters pertaining to women in ministry.

Barbara Heck (1734–1804) founded the first Methodist congregation in America.

Lady Selina Hastings, countess of Huntingdon (1707–1791) who founded the Calvinistic Methodist denomination during the Evangelical Awakening, served as a bishop and appointed Anglican clergymen, assigned their duties, and financed them for several decades. She also founded Trevecca House, a seminary to train ministers for various denominations.[1]

In 1739, John Wesley appointed women as "class leaders" in Bristol. Sarah Mallet received the right hand of fellowship, and Wesley had no objections to her being a preacher as long as she preached the Methodist doctrines and attended to the denomination's discipline.[2]

Nineteenth Century Conservative Reaction

Women in contemporary times have continued to demonstrate gallant efforts like women of past centuries. Despite the conservative reaction to women in the late nineteenth century because of revivalism and frontier egalitarianism, women were catapulted into leadership roles. With great waves of immigration from Europe to America in the nineteenth century, few women were motivated to assume preaching ministries. However, women displayed resilience and tenacity in making their wishes known.

The conservative response that emerged in the latter part of the nineteenth century was due mainly to the effects of industrialization and urbanization that resulted in an erosion of the ideals of marriage and family life. Men were not only robbed of their vocational identity, which required prowess and great physical strength prior to industrialization, but also their absenteeism at home increased. The work place was strictly a male domain to solidify their positions as breadwinners. Women were excluded from business, labor, politics, and government. As a result, women acquired greater influence in the home that replaced the church as the primary religious institution of society. Grenz and Kjesbo noted that religion became largely a female matter as the home became the primary religious institution.[3] As a result, male church leaders grappled with surmounting difficulties in constructing a semblance of the traditional masculine identity. Many fundamentalist clergymen strove to promote male leadership and to curtail the presence of women in positions of authority and their involvement in the public arena.[4]

This conservatism resulted in stiff opposition to the Deaconess Movement in the United States of America, which was in stark contrast to the situation in Germany where the movement started in the nineteenth century and in England to which it spread. In Germany, women were given the opportunity to minister in various places, for example, in hospitals, teacher training centers, programs for rehabilitation of female criminals, homes for the mentally ill, orphanages, facilities for homeless women, and high schools for younger women. In England, the Deaconess Movement was regarded as a type of religious order. In the United States, the movement required celibacy for serving God, contrary to the ideals of American Protestantism and those of women who were devoted to home and family.[5]

Contributions of Women Leaders as Pioneers

Despite the conservative reaction to women leaders in ministry, God continued to raise up modern-day women to leadership positions and to train them for His work in the ministry. Women created platforms for speaking and for being heard. They were founders and leaders of many significant movements for social and religious reforms in the nineteenth and early twentieth century. They became involved in various activist movements to address such issues as suffrage, abolition, and temperance. In the temperance movement, for example, although women were the backbone of this movement, mostly men were in charge of the early organizations. This situation did not permit suitable platforms for women to speak as was the case in the World's Temperance Convention in New York City in 1853. Antoinette Brown, a delegate from her local society, wished to speak but was silenced for several hours.[6]

Women's organizations sprang up everywhere. The most notable one was the Women's Christian Temperance Union (WCTU) founded by Frances Willard. In heeding her call to Christian ministry, she sought the opportunity to address social concerns, specifically, the evils of liquor that destroyed families. Ms. Willard supported the equality of women and men and spoke out in favor of women in church leadership. She served in the church as a source of encouragement to younger women to heed their call to the ministry. In the Temperance organization, women served to evangelize soldiers, sailors, and lumbermen and taught Bible studies in prisons, police stations, and railroad terminals.[7]

Sarah Grimké (1792–1873) was one of the most notable Quaker abolitionists. She and her younger sister Angelina were the daughters of a South Carolina slaveholder and developed an intense dislike for slavery. They moved to Philadelphia to join the Quakers and became very active in the antislavery campaign. The Quakers promoted a platform for women in their assemblies. Soon they became prominent abolitionist speakers, initially at women's circles in private homes and then in churches and halls where they addressed both men and women. As they toured New England in

1837, the General Association of Congregational Ministers of Massachusetts was appalled at women serving as public reformers and addressed mixed audiences of men and women on controversial issues such as abolition and the rights of women as full and equal moral beings. The ministers issued a letter with arguments based on the Bible to oppose women performing roles as public reformers and moral leaders that were traditionally reserved for men.[8]

Sarah Grimké's "Letters on the Equality of the Sexes and the Conditions of Women" (1837–1838) were written one decade before the Seneca Falls Convention of 1848, which was regarded as the formal beginning of the nineteenth-century women's movement. She addressed these letters to her friend, Mary Parker, president of the Boston Anti-Slavery Society, in response to the Congregationalist ministers' rebuke. Although she did not have a formal theological education, she used scripture to support her response for equality of the sexes. The following are some excerpts from the ministers' letter and her responses to them. One excerpt was, "We invite your attention to the dangers which at present seem to threaten the FEMALE CHARACTER with widespread and permanent injury." Grimké believed that if women were to investigate this danger, they would discover that danger [was] pending from those who [had], for a long time, held the reins of usurped authority and who [were] unwilling to allow women to fill the sphere that God intended them to move in, and [had] colluded to crush the immortal mind of woman.[9]

Another excerpt read, "The appropriate duties and influences of women are clearly stated in the New Testament. These duties are unobtrusive and private, but the sources of *mighty power*. When the mild, *dependent*, softening influence of woman upon the sternness of man's opinions is fully exercised, society feels the effects of it in a thousand ways." Grimké strongly desired women to move in the sphere that God assigned them to and believed that their displacement from that sphere resulted in confusion in the world. She alluded to the false interpretation of some passages (of scripture) by men and to the faulty interpretation in their commentaries. She used the Sermon on the Mount to boost her argument for equality of the sexes by noting that Jesus Christ laid down some grand principles for both men and women to follow.[10]

The ministers' letter also stated, "The power of woman is in her dependence, flowing from a consciousness of that weakness which God has given her for her protection." Grimké was willing to acquiesce if this weakness referred to physical weakness pitted against the superior brute force of men. She refuted any claim of mental or moral weakness because she felt that men [had] crushed the powers of [the] minds of women, and their sense of morality [had been] impaired by man's interpretation of their duties. She believed that God did not make any distinction between man and woman as moral and intelligent beings. Lastly, the General Association of Congregationalist Ministers' letter said, "When woman assumes the place and tone of man as a public reformer, our care and protection of her seem unnecessary; we put ourselves in self-defense against her, and her character becomes unnatural." Grimké regarded this statement as making a distinction between the duties of men and women as moral beings. She concluded that what [was] virtue for man [was] vice for woman, and that women who dared to follow the command of Jehovah were threatened with having the protection of the brethren withdrawn.[11]

Women Preachers of the Nineteenth and Twentieth Centuries

Women preachers in the nineteenth and twentieth centuries operated in the gifts of the fivefold ministry despite strong opposition from their male counterparts. In the nineteenth century, the church did not formally recognize many of them through ordination. Many women who served as itinerant evangelists preached in several interdenominational congregations, especially congregations where there were no ordained clergymen. Some of these women preachers pioneered congregations but were replaced by permanent male pastors after the congregations were established and began to flourish. Women continued to function in the fringe sectors of religious life, for example, among the Quakers, Free Methodists, Freewill Baptists, and the Deeper Life movements. Notable among these women was Catherine Booth, Phoebe Palmer, Aimee Semple McPherson, Seth Cook Rees, Carrie Judd Montgomery, and Maria B. Woodworth-Etier.

Catherine Booth (1829–1890) founded the Christian Revival Association in 1865 and the Salvation Army with her husband William Booth in 1878. She was believed to be the more dynamic preacher out of the two. Mrs. Booth started preaching when she was still a Methodist before 1865 and, due to her husband's ill health, sometimes assumed full responsibility for his preaching circuit. She preached her last sermon to an audience of fifty thousand people. Despite her untiring service to God, her husband William

Booth was acknowledged as the founder of the Salvation Army on its official stationery. Even though the Booths believed in the importance of the active participation of women in ministry and the Salvation Army has a long history of men and women sharing leadership roles and of affording both sexes the opportunity to advance, there were some internal struggles with respect to the roles of women.[12]

Phoebe Palmer (1807–1874) was considered "the mother of the Holiness movement." In the late nineteenth century, the participation of women in ministry was welcome in the Holiness churches with the holiness renewal. Phoebe Palmer's ministry began in 1835 and spanned thirty-nine years. She endorsed the right of women to preach, held Tuesday meetings for the promotion of holiness, and served as an inspiration to other women to establish a similar type of ministry throughout North America. As a result, many women leaders sprang up among the Methodists, Congregationalists, Episcopalians, Baptists, and Quakers. She and her husband, Walter Palmer, held successful evangelistic revival meetings in the summer months in such places as New York City, England, and Hamilton, Ontario, in the fall of 1857 and gained several converts in these meetings. It is believed that Mrs. Palmer led over twenty-five thousand converts to Christ.[13]

Aimee Semple McPherson (1890–1944), perhaps the most notable woman evangelist of the twentieth century, was founder of the International Church of the Four-Square Gospel Church, while Seth Cook Rees was cofounder of the Pilgrim Holiness Church. Aimee Semple McPherson believed that Jesus Christ is the same yesterday, today, and forever. She developed a ministry of healing. She believed that even a woman should not resist God's will for her life. However, although these holiness groups officially recognized shared leadership of men and women in the church, their enthusiasm for women leaders waned eventually.[14]

The Pentecostal Movement of the nineteenth century saw such notable women as Maria B. Woodsworth-Etier and Carrie Judd Montgomery. Maria B. Woodsworth-Etier, formerly of the Holiness Movement, became known as an early Pentecostal leader. She was licensed to preach by the Church of God in 1884. Shortly afterward, she began to receive national press coverage and was in great demand to preach. She founded the Woodworth-Etier Tabernacle in Western Indianapolis in 1918, which she pastored until her death in 1924.[15]

Carrie Judd Montgomery was a renowned healing evangelist who cofounded the Christian and Missionary Alliance in 1887 with A. B.

Simpson. She participated in the Pentecostal Revival and was ordained as a minister by the Assemblies of God Church in 1917. Her ministry lasted until 1946.[16]

There were also some notable black women leaders in the nineteenth century in the United States of America. Such leaders included Jarena Lee, Zilpha Elaw, and Julia Foote from the Methodist tradition. They claimed their authority to preach through the scriptures. Contributing to their own authority were their personal interpretation of scripture, their experience of voices and visions, and their ability to hear the voice of God. Through vision, they were assured of the leading of God on their lives.

Julia Foote was born in Schenectady, New York, of former slaves. She received very little formal education between ages ten and twelve after she was hired by a white family as a domestic servant. She read the Bible profusely and was profoundly converted at age fifteen. She joined an African Methodist Episcopal Church in Albany, New York. Julia Foote interpreted her relationship with God through her reading of scripture. She believed in the doctrine of sanctification in which a person could be completely freed from sin and empowered to lead a life of spiritual perfection. This doctrine was a controversial debate in Methodists circles for several decades. She believed that she was sanctified by the Holy Spirit and destined to preach the Gospel of Christ. She was fully aware that a woman's claim of divine calling to ministry contradicted Christian tradition and American social prejudice. Women were not allowed to assume public leadership positions, and their opportunity to speak in public was restricted. Initially, she did some informal evangelistic work in her community. Subsequently, she was denied access to a pulpit ministry in Boston and set out on an independent preaching career. She evangelized the upstate New York region in the mid-1840s and went in search of new converts in Ohio and Michigan in the 1850s. She participated in the holiness revivals in the 1870s and then became a missionary in the A. M. E. Zion Church. She was the first woman to be ordained as a deacon and the second woman elder in her denomination.[17]

Zilpha Elaw preached and ministered through the Holy Spirit who loved and indwelt her.

Jarena Lee preached in the African Methodist Episcopal Church. Her calling was realized through her experience of voice. She consulted with a minister who informed her that the Methodists did not allow women to preach. Four or five years after her "sanctification," she heard a voice telling her to go and preach the Gospel. Although the African Methodist Episcopal

Church did not permit women to preach, Jarena Lee contended that since nothing was impossible with God, it should not be considered impossible or improper for a woman to preach the Gospel. She based her reasoning on the fact that the Savior died for both man and woman and that both man and woman should preach. She referenced Mary as the first to preach about the resurrection of the crucified Son of God. She supported this view by saying that even if some people (might) argue that Mary did not expound the scripture, preaching might have been much simpler in those days than it is now since unlearned fishermen could not have preached the Gospel. She believed that preaching the Gospel came solely by inspiration and that God could inspire a female to preach the simple story of the birth, life, death, and resurrection of our Lord and accompany it with power to the sinner's heart. She was fully persuaded that God had called her to labor in His vineyard, which was consistently confirmed by the awakening and converting of sinners. She was firmly convinced that her labor would be rewarded in the great day of accounts.[18] Both she and Zilpha Elaw were very comfortable speaking with this voice from which precious truth was obtained. Jarena Lee argued in support of the right of women to preach. For her, Jesus Christ died for all humanity. She regarded the humanity of Christ with paramount importance rather than the maleness of God, hence the justification of both male and female preaching.[19] Finally, with the approval of her bishop, she moved from "exhortation" to full preaching and was able to impact the lives of many African-American and whites profoundly in her travels.

Women Leaders of the Twentieth Century

In the twentieth century, women continued to strive for full recognition as capable ministers in the Christian community. Many women served in the capacity of leaders and were used mightily by God in the fivefold ministry. The following list is merely a sample of outstanding women leaders who labored in ministry in the United States of America, Canada, and Europe.

Pioneers of the Pentecostal Movement

At the beginning of the twentieth century, Florence L. Crawford was a part of the early Pentecostal Renewal in the United States of America through her itinerant ministry. She planted and pastored several churches in the Pacific Northwest. She founded the Apostolic Faith Church, subsequently known as Open Bible Standard denomination that was based in Portland, Oregon, and served as its general overseer.

Other women who performed leadership roles as pioneers in the United States of America were Mabel Smith; Ivey Campbell; Rachel A. Sizelove; Maud Williams; Mrs. Scott Ladd, founder of a Pentecostal Mission in 1907; the Duncan Sisters, founders of the Rochester Bible Training School at Elim Faith Home; "Mother" Barnes who conducted tent meetings in Southern Illinois (1908); Marie Burgess, founder of the Glad Tidings Hall from which the Pentecostal Revival grew; and Kathryn Kuhlman.

Kathryn Kuhlman was considered one of the world's most renowned healing evangelists. She began her ministry in 1923 and was subsequently ordained by the Evangelical Church Alliance of Illinois. She founded Denver Revival Tabernacle in 1935, which she pastored for three years. She subsequently became a preacher and radio evangelist in Franklin, Pennsylvania, in the 1940s. She was a pinnacle of the Charismatic Movement until her death in 1976.

In Canada, some notable pioneers were Ella M. Goff of Winnipeg, Ellen Hebden of Toronto, Alice B. Garrigus of NewFoundland, the Davis sisters of the Maritime Provinces, Zelma Argue throughout Canada, C. E. Baker of Montreal, Aimee Semple McPherson of Ingersoll, Ontario, who began her preaching ministry in Toronto in 1915 and carried the Gospel across the United States in 1918. She founded Angelus Temple in 1923 and served there as senior pastor until her death in 1944.

In England, Jesse Penn Lewis was a renowned authoress and minister and a participant of the Pentecostal revival in Wales.

In the 1960s and 1970s, several notable Pentecostal pastors, evangelists, authors, and speakers emerged in the Charismatic Movement. Some of these pastors were Charlotte Baker, Myrtle D. Beale, Aimee Cortese, Sue Curran, Helen Beard, Hattie Hammond, Alpha A. Henson, Marilyn Hickey, Freda Lindsay, Iverna Tompkins, and Rachel Titus. Some speakers, evangelists, or authors were Eleanor and Roberta Armstrong, Rita Bennett, Edith Blomhofer, Hazel Bonawitz, Roxanne Brant, Mary Ann Brown, Shirley Carpenter, Daisy Osborn, Agnes Sandford, Given Shaw, Bernice Smith, Ruth Carter Stapleton, and Jean Stone.[20]

Women Leaders of the Twenty-First Century

Present-day bastions of the faith include world-renowned leaders such as Joyce Meyer, Taffi Dollar, Kay Arthur, Lindsay Roberts, Gloria Copeland, Paula White, and Pat Francis.

Renowned charismatic teacher, author, televangelist, and humanitarian Joyce Meyer became involved in part-time ministry in 1976 and full-time ministry in 1980. As an associate pastor in the Life Christian Church in St. Louis, Missouri, she initiated a weekly meeting known as "Life in the Word" until she was directed by God to launch her own ministry currently known as Life in the Word Inc. Her *Enjoying Everyday Life* TV program is aired on BET. Her ministry is headquartered in Fenton, Missouri. Her radio and television conferences are aired in thirty languages, in two hundred countries the world over, and she travels extensively to hold Life in the Word conferences. Her partners in ministry are her husband, Dave Meyer, the business administrator of Life in the Word, her four children, and their spouses. She has recorded over two hundred audiocassettes and dozens of videos and has written approximately ninety books to equip the body of Christ.[21]

Pastor Taffi Dollar is copastor of World Changers Church International, a congregation of over twenty-thousand people with her husband, Dr. Creflo Dollar, who founded the World Changers Christian Center, College Park, Georgia. She actively participates in the *Changing Your World* broadcasts via television and radio and is a well-renowned author, teacher, and conference speaker. She has a global influence in ministry and music and serves as the CEO of Arrow Records, a Christian recording company. She conducts conferences in the United States and around the world and is vice president of the ministry and overseer of the women's fellowship. She founded the Women's Ministry to promote unity and sisterhood and the Prestige Ministry to reach out to women involved in the adult entertainment and sex-trade industries.[22]

Kay Arthur is a famous international Bible teacher on radio. She and her husband, Jack Arthur, were two missionaries in Mexico who returned to Chattanooga, USA, in the late 1960s due to impaired health. She started a Bible study for teenagers in her living room and soon this ministry expanded to include adults. She founded Precept Ministries International as it is currently known. It is a transdenominational organization that has spread to over one hundred countries, resulting in thousands of people being reached daily and weekly through "Precept upon Precept" study series. She takes her authority from the Word of God and uses the inductive study method in helping others to know the Word of God and to apply it to their daily lives. She founded Transform Student Ministries, an outreach of Precept Ministries International to high school–aged and college-aged students. She has a very effective writing and teaching ministry and is the author of over one hundred books and Bible studies. She is four-time ECPA Christian Book Award-winning author. [23]

Lindsay Roberts was married to Richard Roberts in 1980 and since that time has traveled the world over with her husband to do God's work. Together, they have coauthored many books and have established and overseen more than two hundred ministries. She has also written several children's books. She is editor of a semiannual daily devotion periodical called *Daily Blessing: Make Your Day Count*, a quarterly magazine for women, and *Miracles Now*, a bimonthly magazine for ministry partners. She is host of a television show entitled *Make Your Day Count*. She cohosts a nightly television program, *The Hour of Healing* with her husband, Richard Roberts, and is a dynamic preacher.[24]

Gloria Copeland is an author and Christian minister who is involved in shared ministry with her husband, Kenneth Copeland, both of whom preach and teach the Word of God and address such issues as love, faith, healing, prosperity, righteousness, and the anointing. She cofounded Kenneth Copeland Ministries with her husband Kenneth Copeland in 1967. Kenneth Copeland Ministries, also known as Eagle Mountain International Church, has been bringing the news of Jesus Christ around the world for several decades. Gloria Copeland speaks in meetings all over the world and cohosts the daily *Believer's Voice of Victory* television program with her husband. She and her husband have authored dozens of books. She has written many best-selling books and was selected as Christian Woman of the Year by the Christian Woman of the Year Association in 1994.[25]

Paula White was copastor and cofounder with her former husband, Dr. Randy White of Without Walls International Church, formerly South Tampa Christian Center, which they founded in 1991. This has been a fast growing, culturally diverse, and multiracial congregation of approximately twelve thousand people in Tampa, Florida. Evangelist Paula White has been in charge of the ladies ministry, Women of the Word. As host of the *Paula White Show*, she recorded her first broadcast in December 2001. She authored *He Loves Me, He Loves Me Not*. She founded Operation

Explosion, a weekly ministry to the inner city project areas, and has led thousands of souls to Christ through conferences, crusades, and retreats. She exhorts and motivates through her dynamic preaching and teaching. In July 2009, she replaced her former husband, Randy White, as senior pastor of Without Walls International Church, Tampa, Florida, and in January 2011, she became senior pastor of Without Walls Central Church in Lakeland, Florida, making her the senior pastor of both the Tampa and Lakeland locations.[26]

Dr. Pat Francis obtained a doctor of ministry degree from Christian Life School in Columbus, Georgia, USA, and holds a doctorate in Psychotherapy Counseling. She became the founding pastor of Deeper Life Christian Ministries, currently known as Kingdom Covenant Ministries, in 1999 in Mississauga, Ontario, Canada, which now has a weekly attendance of over three thousand people. She demonstrates a burning passion, zeal, and commitment to changing the lives of troubled children and youth. She is president of Acorn to Youth Services, which helps at-risk youth and young adults in need of academic, social, and judicial help. She has been recognized and honored with several awards in Canada and the United States of America for her many initiatives and programs that provide solutions for youth and the community. Compassion for the Poor, the humanitarian arm of Pat Francis Ministries, assists communities in missions-relief help to the poor, orphanages, and medical centers, as well as provides teaching and training to people in order to eradicate systematic poverty and create solutions for systematic prosperity. She is CEO of the Elomax Group of for-profit companies with a vision to create wealth and provide solutions for the poor. She travels the world over to share the life-transforming message of hope and power. She is also an author of several inspiring transformational books and has published over 125 motivational CD and DVD titles.[27]

Women Leaders in Missions in the Nineteenth and Twentieth Centuries

Women's Movements

Many women's missionary movements came into existence in the nineteenth and twentieth centuries. Missionary boards still were not open to sending women on the mission field although women assumed a more significant role than men in the mission movement for approximately fifty years, following the Civil War in the United States of America. As a result, women decided to organize their own boards. The first of these boards was the Women's Union Missionary Society. At home, these boards built women's colleges where women were trained for missionary service. Approximately, one thousand women's missionary societies came into existence locally. In the local churches, their function was to pray and to raise funds to build hospitals and schools the world over and to send single women on the mission field as doctors, teachers, and evangelists. However, after the women's missionary boards amalgamated with the denominational boards in the 1920s and 1930s, women lost control of these boards.[28]

Yonggi Cho believed that women are better suitable for difficult pioneering work because they never give up. They persevere when men are discouraged. He felt that men are good builders of missionary work.[29] Like Yonggi Cho, there were three other famous men who supported women as missionaries. These men were Hudson Taylor, D. L. Moody, and Fredrick Franson.

Hudson Taylor used women as missionaries, which he believed that God directed him to do. He had a strong relationship with God and was the founder of Inland China Mission. He felt that it was crucial to recruit women and send them to evangelize cross-culturally. Initially, he expected both married and single women to perform all missionary duties, including preaching and teaching.[30]

D. L. Moody also encouraged women in Christian service. Frances Willard, founder of the World Women's Christian Temperance Union, served for some time as an assistant to Moody and wrote *Woman in the Pulpit* in defense of the ministry of women. He had a strong relationship with and faith in God. His conviction was that all Christians should go to work.

Fredrick Franson was a Swedish immigrant who was influenced by D. L. Moody and became the first commissioned missionary of Moody's congregation. He brought revival to many European countries and to many missionary societies. Through his and J. Hudson Taylor's encouragement, China became an extremely fruitful field for the ministry of women. Franson founded the Evangelical Alliance Mission. Wherever he went, the majority of the congregation consisted of women. He strongly felt that women should assist in the evangelization of the world. As a result, he wrote a little book on women and the evangelization of the world entitled *Prophesying Daughters*. Originally, this book was written in German and subsequently translated into Swedish.[31]

Examples of Women Leaders in Missionary Activities

In the early missionary movement, most Protestant women who went to the mission field were wives of missionaries. Men soon realized that women were more effective missionaries to women in non-Western societies. With the encouragement of male leaders such as A. B. Simpson, A. J. Gordon who endorsed women's gifts for public ministry, D. L. Moody, J. Hudson Taylor, and Fredrick Franson, doors were opened for single women to evangelize the world. Although such women did not necessarily have a commitment to singleness by taking vows of celibacy, many of them chose to remain single because of a scarcity of male missionaries or because the Christian ideals of their suitors did not match theirs or because their suitors were unsuitable for or disinterested in missionary activities.[32] Also, many women chose to remain single because of the female agencies that sent them to the mission field and provided their travel expenses and support on the mission field.

With regard to the women's missionary movement, Beaver noted that it was "built upon a celibate order of life career missionaries, maintained on a subsistence level." They were expected to remain celibate in service for life, and if they chose to marry or to forsake their commission in any other way, they were forced to return their travel and outfit allowances and sometimes their salaries in keeping with a signed pledge.[33]

Most of these women who took to the mission field were bound by a deep sense of commitment to God that transcended the attainment of personal recognition or power.[34] Their enthusiasm and motivation kindled a fire in the hearts of other women in the home churches for world vision. Women such as Annie Armstrong and Helen Barret Montgomery dedicated their time, energy, money, and organizational skill to raising funds and mobilizing Christians to support missions. They developed missionary prayer groups in support of their female allies in foreign lands.

Henrietta Mears who was called Teacher by thousands of her students at Hollywood Presbyterian Church, USA, was a significant leader who prepared people for missionary activities. She taught many outstanding men such as Bill Bright, founder of Campus Crusade for Christ, and Richard Halverson, pastor of South Presbyterian Church, Washington, DC. She challenged young men to the ministry and, under her tutelage, over four hundred of her students took to pulpits in America or to mission stations the world over. She founded Gospel Lighthouse Publications where high-quality Christian Education material was produced. She served as a professor of

Christian Education at Fuller Theological Seminary and thousands of people studied the Bible under her leadership.

There is a rich heritage of women in missions of which the following are worthy of mention. Cynthia Farrar in India and Elizabeth Agnew in Ceylon were among many single women who supervised women's schools. They helped in zenanas and harems or in medical service.

Charlotte Diggs "Lottie" Moon (1840–1912) was referred to as the "patron saint" of the Southern Baptists. She turned down a marriage proposal by Crawford Toy, a confederate army chaplain, despite bouts of loneliness in China because his Christian ideals were contrary to hers. He was a Darwinian evolutionist and Moon did not regard evolution as tenable. At home in America, she wielded tremendous influence in missionary outreach and in giving. She took to China in 1873 where she initially taught in a children's school. Eventually, she took to evangelism and church planting among the Chinese people after viewing herself as a part of the oppressed class of single-women missionaries since she was saddled with the petty work of teaching a few girls. She expressed the sentiments of contemporary women who are hindered from realizing their full potential in ministry. She strongly believed that women had the right to use their God-given gifts in ministry to the fullest capacity and fought for equality in ministry for the oppressed class of women. Despite initial opposition from her field instructor, she succeeded in doing evangelistic work, and in fact, she evangelized at P'ing-Tu Center. This center was considered the greatest evangelistic center among the Southern Baptists in China. She mobilized resources for the recruitment of single women missionaries in China.[35]

Malla Moe was one of the longest-serving and most fruitful missionaries in South Africa where she ministered to both males and females. Originally from Norway, she emigrated to the United States of America and was profoundly influenced by D. L. Moody who exhorted Christians to go to work and by Fredrick Franson who told her God wanted her to go to Africa. She subsequently joined the Evangelical (formerly Scandinavian) Alliance Mission that Franson had founded to enlist Scandinavians to go to Japan and South Africa as missionaries.[36]

Amy Carmichael was born in Ireland in 1867 and initially went to Japan as a missionary at age twenty-six. She returned to Great Britain in less than two years due to ill health. At age twenty-eight, she went to Bangalore, India, where the climate was considered more conducive to her health. She began her ministry by traveling to several villages with several Indian sisters to spread the Gospel. She spent fifty-three years in India where she founded the Sisters of Common Life and where she wrote thirty-five books to give details of her contributions in India. She was deeply struck by the vice of temple prostitution after a seven-year-old girl Preena escaped from the temple in 1901 and sought her help. This was the beginning of a work later known as Dohnavur Fellowship. Initially, she rescued both boys and girls from the jaws of prostitution.

Dohnavur is located in Tamil Nadu, approximately thirty miles from the tip of India. It is not an orphanage, but a family of individuals who assume life membership under the family name Carunia, Tamil for "loving kindness." Members of this family are the retired housemothers, many of whom have raised dozens of children over the years. A legacy of laborers lives on. Today, an all-Indian staff mans the Fellowship.[37]

Marie Monsen originally came from Norway and labored in China from the 1920s. She had the knack to expose sin within the church, even among church leaders and among the Chinese. She met a Danish missionary and his wife, the Jensens in Manchuria, China, where they had been working for thirty years and was able to actively participate in the revival there. She traveled inland to Peking where she participated in many missionary efforts and witnessed a mighty moving of God. Her ministry met with great opposition in Manchuria and Peking, partly by some male missionaries. However, the prayers of intercessors supported her, and eventually the walls of opposition crumbled.[38]

Naomi Dowdy went to Singapore in October 1975 to work as an evangelist and to make it the base for her evangelistic activities in Asia. Instead, a Chinese church asked her to be its pastor. By 1985, the members of that church had multiplied by leaps and bounds, from forty-nine in 1975 to two thousand members. She started a theological center in rented quarters.

In Puerto Rico, in the 1970s, Luz M. Dones de Reyes was called to pastor a Baptist congregation of twelve. Ten years later, her congregation had grown to nine hundred and was considered in those days to be the largest rural congregation in Puerto Rico. In the 1980s, female pastors of exceptional caliber were in charge of four Puerto Rican Baptist churches.[39]

The following were other contemporary women leaders in missions: Gladys Aylward, an English servant girl, served as a missionary among Chinese men who included rough-pack mule drivers, military officials, and Mandarins. Irene Webster-Smith worked in Japan in a children's orphanage, and later, she worked among top Japanese war crime prisoners, many of whom she led to Christ before their execution.⁴⁰ Elizabeth Elliot served many years among the Auca tribe (Huaorani) in Ecuador, following the spearing to death of her husband, Jim Elliot, and four of his coworkers. She wrote approximately twenty books that dealt with a variety of issues, such as God's plan for the Christian family, suffering, loneliness, and Christian dating. She performed a significant role in frontier mission and stressed that it takes a deep spiritual encounter with the cross before one is really qualified to call oneself a missionary.⁴¹ Mary Slessor was a pioneer in Africa; Amy Judson in Burma, Rosalind Goforth in China, Mildred Gobi in the Gobi Desert, Eliza Davis George, black woman missionary, to Liberia, and Isobel Kuhn, a missionary to China and an author.

The list of these precious women continue to be impressive even as some conservative theologians, ministers, and other members of the church community continue to debate whether women are called by God to certain leadership roles. Women leaders from different lands and of different tongues, racial, cultural, and religious backgrounds have proven their success in missions in such areas as church planting, teaching, preaching the Gospel, establishing training schools, supervising building projects, erecting and directing hospitals, and evangelization.⁴² Women are dynamic in the fivefold ministry around the world as the Holy Spirit works in their lives to perform the tasks He has chosen them to perform. They will continue to be used mightily of God, defying all odds, critics, skeptics, and conservatives who may never be silenced.

Contemporary Women's Movements

Women's movements have been in existence for centuries, but in contemporary times, they took shape and form from the days of the Enlightenment and the French Revolution when women attempted to free themselves from bondage to become who they truly were, both inwardly and outwardly. From its inception, the contemporary women's movement took place in the secular realm. Its purpose was twofold. One aspect of the movement was started by middle-class women who caught the vision of the Enlightenment that focused on the power of reason. Women clamored for education and schooling so that they could attain maturity as humans could realize their full potential and exercise their right to become their true selves. As a result, women founded colleges for training women as school mistresses, kindergarten teachers, and social workers.

This middle-class movement was accompanied by another kind of women's movement known as the working-class movement of men and women, a workers' movement. It struck at the core of the liberation of women to economic independence. In his book, *Die frau und der sozialismus* (Women under Socialism), August Bebel highlighted the double oppression of women, which is their economic dependence on men and men's access to their bodies. Women were educated to obey (men). Bebel advocated freedom for women through the abolition of the class system and for the emergence of a new society with equal rights for women (and men). He believed that women should be liberated to participate in the production process.

The church was ambivalent about the women's movements. On one hand, it opposed the movements. On the other hand, some church circles afforded young girls their first educational opportunities. As well, women in the church began to pay attention to what the secular women's movements were trying to accomplish or had accomplished.

In referring to the period between what she considered to be the earlier women's movements and the modern women's movements, which began around the 1960s in the United States of America, Bührig believed that denominational and ecumenical women's organizations were not only alerted to the struggles of the secular women's movements, but joined in those struggles, especially between the end of the Second World War and 1970. She based her opinion partly on her examination of female authors such as Elisabeth Gössmann, Elisabeth Schüssler Fiorenza of the 1960s, lectures of Basel theologian, Dorothee Hoch, published in 1959 under the title of *Weg und aufgabe der frau heute* (The Way and Task of Woman Today) and Charlotte von Kirschbaum's book, *Die wirkliche frau* (The Real Woman) of 1949. She was also impressed that the World Council of Churches, at its inaugural World Assembly in Amsterdam in 1948, had set up a commission on the "Life and Task of Women in the Church." A French woman named Madeleine Barot of the Reformed Church spearheaded this project to inquire into the roles and functions of women in the church. Kathleen Bliss published the results of this commission. The formation of the Commission of the World Council of Churches was a progress in the cause of women who struggled to find a voice in the church universally. From the 1960s, women in the United States of America continued the struggle in "the second wave of the women's movements." At that time, women were seeking for a profound change in society and for the freedom of all humanity.[43]

The following quote from Dorothee Sölle strikes at the core of this movement and sheds light on what women are truly in search of:

> *We do not want*
> *to become like men*
> *in our society*
> *crippled beings*
> *under pressure to achieve*
> *emotionally impoverished*
> *made into bureaucratic objects*
> *pushed into specialization*
> *condemned to make a career . . .*
> *We do not want*
> *to learn what men can*
> *to dominate and to command*
> *to be served and to conquer*
> *to hunt to exploit to subdue*[44]

Let women continue to be women, but let them be liberated to exercise the right, power, and authority bestowed on them by the Holy Spirit for service in the body of Christ. No more hindrances! No more setting of limits on God and women! No more restrictions! With critics and skeptics on every hand to hinder the growth of women, their struggle to achieve their rightful places in ministry and to erase the stigma of taking second place to their male counterparts and to work in true partnership with them persists. Women are not seeking to wield power over men in a sinister, inappropriate, or power-drunk fashion or to embrace the thirst for "masculine" power or to condone ongoing dependency on their male counterparts. They are simply trying to coexist with men and to carve out a real identity for themselves in the body of Christ. Women must be liberated to wing their flight to higher spiritual realms and to experience their full potential as leaders.

---

1. Richard M. Riss, A Brief History of Women in Ministry [Online] available http://www.bible.com/answers/awomemin.html (22/04/2001), 12–13.
2. Dorothy R. Pape, *In Search of God's Ideal Woman: A Personal Examination of the New Testament* (Downers Grove, Illinois 60515: InterVarsity Press, 1977), 227–228.

3. Stanley Grenz with Denise Muir Kjesbo, *Women in the Church: A Biblical Theology of Women in Ministry* (Downers Grove, Illinois: InterVarsity Press, 1995), 47–46.
4. Ibid., 48–49.
5. Ibid., 49.
6. Ibid., 50–51.
7. Ibid.
8. Ibid.
9. Elizabeth A. Clarke and Herbert Richardson, eds. *Women and Religion: The Original Sourcebook of Women in Christian Thought* (San Francisco: Harper, 1996), 237–245.
10. Ibid.
11. Ibid.
12. Grenz with Kjesbo, op. cit., 53–54.
13. Riss, op. cit., 13–14.
14. Ibid.
15. Ibid.
16. Ibid.
17. William L. Andrews, "Julia A. J. Foote (1823–1900)" [Online] Available http://college.hmco.com/english/lauter/heath/4e/student/author_pages/late_nineteenth/foot, 1
18. Clarke and Richardson, eds., op. cit., 258–259.
19. Nantawan Boonprasat Lewis, et al, *Sisters Struggling in the Spirit: A Women of Color Theological Anthology* (Louisville, Kentucky: Women's Ministries Program Area, National Ministries Division, Presbyterian Church (USA), 1994), 31–40, 188–189.
20. Riss, op. cit., 14–15.
21. "Joyce Meyer" [Online] Available http://www.twbookmark.com/authors/20/2594/ (1/4/2003), also in Wikipedia.org.
22. Dr. Creflo A. Dollar and his wife, Pastor Taffi Dollar [Online] Available http://www.cfaith.com/Cfaith/SUPPORT/biography affiliate/O.3909.109,00.asp (1/4/2003), also in Creflo and Taffi Dollar—Christian Author Profile, http://www.faithcentredresources.com/authors/creflo-taffi-dollar.asp (1/4/2003), 1.
23. Kay Arthur [Online] Available www.precept.org/about.html, also in "Kay Arthur—Cofounder of Precept Ministries International, www.preceptflorida.org/Kayarthur.htm, also in wikipedia.org.
24. Lindsay Roberts [Online] Available www.orm.cc/bio_lr.html.
25. Harrison House: About Kenneth & Gloria Copeland [Online] Available, also in wikipedia.org. http://www.harrisonhouse.com/AuthorInfo.asp?IDA-621 (1/4/2003) 1, also in Welcome to Kenneth Copeland Ministries I About Us, http://www.kcm.org/about/ (1/4/2003), 1.
26. "Dr. Randy A. White, Senior Pastor Without Walls International Church" [Online] Available www.withoutwalls.org/pastor.htm, also in Pastor Paula White Biography, www.honeybzz4u.com/events/paula_white/paula_white.html, also in wikipedia.org.
27. "Pat Francis Biography" [Online] Available http://www.patfrancis.org/biography.htm, also in http://patfrancis.org/pf_bio.php.

28. Marguerite Kraft and Meg Crossman, "Women in Missions" *Mission Frontiers* (August 1999), The US Center for World Mission 21: 5–8, 16.
29. Ibid., in Paul Yonggi Cho at El Shaddai Pastors Fellowship luncheon in Phoenix, Az. March 1988.
30. Ibid., 15.
31. Pape, op. cit., 231–234.
32. Kraft and Crossman, op. cit., 15.
33. Ibid., in R. Pierce Beaver, *American Protestant Women in Mission* (Grand Rapids, Michigan: Eerdmans, 1980), 178.
34. Ibid., in Ruth Tucker, *Guardians of the Great Commission* Grand Rapids, Mi: Academic Books, 1988), 38.
35. Ruth Tucker, "Lottie Moon: Saint of the Southern Baptists," ibid., 18–19.
36. Pape, op. cit., 232.
37. Phyllis L. Berry, "A Living Legacy: Amy Carmichael and the Origin of the Dohnavur Fellowship," *Mission Frontiers* (August 1999), 23.
38. Pape, op. cit., 238–244.
39. Bonnidell Clouse and Robert G. Clouse, eds., *Women in Ministry: Four Views* Downers Grove, Illinois 60515: InterVarsity Press, 1989), 179, cited from Alvera Mickelson, "An Egalitarian View: There Is Neither Male nor Female in Christ."
40. Pape, op. cit., 244.
41. Russell G. Shubin, "Strength in the Face of Adversity," *Mission Frontiers* (August 1999), 21.
42. Clouse and Clouse, eds., op. cit., 176–177.
43. Marga Bührig, *Woman Invisible: A Personal Odyssey in Christian Feminism* (Rochester, Kent: Burns & Oates, 1993) 26–32.
44. Ibid., 32, from Dorothee Sölle, *Die revolutionäre Geduld* (Berlin: Fietkau, 1974).

Chapter Six:
Marginalization and Struggles of Women Leaders in Ministry

Marginalization among women leaders in ministry was born in the early church as was noted in the church offices that were held by women leaders in those times. This marginalization was aided and abetted by the institutionalization of the church in the first and second centuries, with the emergence of the all-male priesthood concept, which influenced the ordering of the church throughout the centuries that followed and which resulted in women leaders performing secondary roles and operating in fringe areas of ministry. Women leaders have experienced discrimination in many areas of ministry such as salaries, marital status, job acquisition, job roles and functions, and job promotion. They may be subjected to verbal and sexual harassment. They have been invisible and silenced in the church for centuries and have struggled for full recognition and participation in ministry with their male counterparts.

Marginalization and Early Christian Offices for Women

The earliest form of marginalization reared its ugly and monstrous head in the offices held by women in the church. These offices included the Order of Widows (1 Timothy 5:3–16) and the Office of Deaconess (1 Timothy 3:11).

The Order of Widows came into existence as a result of the cultural barriers that prohibited the integration of the sexes. The widows were female presbyters who performed subordinate duties. Initially, they were restricted to their homes where they were to dedicate themselves to the service of prayer and were forbidden to undertake any religious instruction or to administer the sacraments. Although they were the counterparts of the male presbyters, their rights and activities in the church were progressively restricted. Ida Raming contributed fear as a factor among the male deaconate for the suppression of the female presbyters who posed a serious threat to the presbyterial and episcopal offices. This fear was laid to rest when the Council of Laodicea (343) instituted that women could not be appointed as elders (presbyterae) in the church. Sacramental functions became an all-male prerogative as women were denied any official participation in the life of the church.[1] Women being confined to the fringe areas of service due to fear of their male counterparts could possibly be viewed in the light of present-day attempts to continue the trend of limiting women to fringe positions in ministry. Fear that cripples or results in one sex vying for supremacy in the hierarchical structure of the church runs counter to the leadings of God who has not given believers a spirit of fear but of a sound mind. On the contrary, godly fear emboldens and equips people for the ministry to which God has called them. If, indeed, some male leaders experience fear, this fear does not originate from God but from the desire of man to dominate and from the thirst for power. The Holy Spirit equips us for ministry, and believers must be careful to assume only the ministerial gifts that He bestows upon them.

After the Order of Deaconess was instituted, deaconesses were ordained subsequently to the official ordering of the church, yet their male counterparts held them at bay. They were forced into a cloistered lifestyle and assumed some of the functions previously performed by the widows. These functions resulted in their marginalization as they performed subordinate duties such as the anointing of the bodies of women for reasons of decency for baptism by immersion. The Order of Deaconess met with stiff opposition as demonstrated in the Syrian *Didascalia* in a document known as the *Apostolic Constitutions*, a pseudoapostolic collection of legal and liturgical material from the fourth century.[2] This document spelled out the arguments that "if the man is the head of the woman, then it is not seemly for the rest of the body to rule the head ... That is to say, if the man is the head of the woman and he is called to the priesthood, then it is against all justice to overturn the arrangement made by the Creator and make over to the lowest limb prerogatives which have been granted to the man; for the woman is the man's body, she is made from his rib and put in subjection under him, which is also why she was chosen to bear children."[3]

These arguments indicate a general assumption that only men may be called to the priesthood. It is a misconception to equate subjection to a woman being made from a man's rib, which on the contrary suggests equality. There was further opposition to the Order of Deaconess in decisions of several Gallican synods of the fourth and sixth centuries. Deaconesses were forbidden to be ordained.

Historical Perspectives on Discrimination against Women

Hamilton and Hamilton noted that throughout the history of the Christian church, women have been denied leadership positions, except when they were directed by males. Nevertheless, women have been the mainstay of the practice of Christian life and Christian worship. They have surpassed men in the day-to-day living of the life of faith and in the bequeathing of faith to the next generation.[4] It is no wonder, then, that the majority of adults in many congregations are females, which strategically can present many opportunities for the ministry of women leaders. Seeing also that women perform such a vital role in the propagation of faith, both in the faith community and in the society at large, their influence in ministerial leadership should be accepted and respected for what it is truly worth and should not be denied.

Historically, the part that women played in the ministry of the church and the status of their ministry has never been clearly defined. Although they played a significant part in the early church and continue to make their presence felt in the church today, the pendulum has swung back and forth with regard to defining their status. Pape noted that its form varied with particular times and countries, and a change in its characteristics, subject to different needs. It was either included in the ordained ministry or regarded as a lay activity.[5]

Referring to offices in the early church, Pape questioned the common element of the "one-man ministry" in the average Protestant churches. She emphasized the focus of theologians, when examining women leaders in Paul's Epistles, on whether women actually functioned in official capacities in the early church and rightly concluded that offices are man-made institutions.[6] This being so, focusing on who should hold which offices in the church is destructive and overshadows the true meaning of ministry and its emphasis on serving. It is a petty matter when viewed in the context of the Great Commission given to the church by Christ. There is much work to be done to build God's kingdom and too little time to have such a dissension in the church. Are not men and women chosen to perform leadership functions in the church? Does it really matter who plants and who waters? It is crucial for the church to maintain focus on winning the lost and preparing itself for the return of Christ? Despite the fact that a woman's official status might be uncertain and varied, it did not prevent her from wielding tremendous influence in the early church.

When the church became institutionalized in the first and second centuries, an all-male hierarchical priesthood emerged, resulting in another shift in the exclusion of women from official ministry. In fact, it was a reflection of the inconstant tradition of the exclusion of or attempt to exclude women from official ministry. With institutionalization came the rise and development of male domination in the church as reflected in the characteristics and structural features of the churches.

Raming described male domination in the church by noting that the holders of ecclesiastical offices, including the deaconate, presbyterate, and episcopate were exclusively male. She noted that leadership, pastoral, and other functions involving teaching, legislation, and administration were inextricably linked with the ecclesiastical offices and were constantly exercised by men only. Theological teaching and research were carried out by men who structured the church in such a manner as to confirm and sanction male predominance in the church.[7] This phenomenon was reflected in ecclesiastical language and visual representations. So great were the power and influence of men that women were forced to participate in a very limited way in the pastoral and catechetical works in certain restricted areas of the church's life.[8] Male domination compromised the full humanity of women by placing emphasis on maleness, thus overriding the truism that both male and female were created in the image of God.

Male domination not only fostered limitation of women in ministry but also excluded women from the priesthood. The ecclesiastical structure encouraged segregation of the sexes. The prevailing tradition of women as temptresses resulted in the formation of the Orders of Widows and Deaconesses to provide for the care of women in a manner that was nonthreatening to the purity of the priests. The ministry, which women performed, was limited to women and was considered less important than the ministry of their male counterparts.[9]

Women leaders continued to make their presence felt into the Dark Ages and the centuries beyond. It is believed that the activities of women reached their peak in the fourth century in the early church. Some notable women whose characters stood out were Emmelia, Athusa, Norma, and Monica, whose accomplishments, outstanding piety, and fervor in defending the faith lent credence to the vibrant nature of their ministry. Some of them suffered martyrdom for their faith, such as Blandina, Perpetua, and Felicitas. With the dawn of the Middle Ages, concerted efforts were made by the clergy for whom celibacy had become a prevalent idea to fully seclude women, thus closing all channels to their active ministry. Yet in Medieval Europe, cloistered nuns and abbesses were able to have tremendous social and religious influence in the rural areas (of their countries). Some abbesses succeeded in exercising ecclesiastical and manorial jurisdiction over towns and parishes. Although the cloister was imposed upon all women who officially served the church, this way of life became less common for their male counterparts. However, the spirits of women could not be daunted.[10] They stood firm and true to the calling of God on their lives and kept the light of Christianity ablaze in Medieval Europe.

Church fathers held tremendous influence, and their pronouncements were regarded as virtually infallible and given preeminence over the decisions of councils or ordinances of the Pope, especially pertaining to the exposition of scripture. The church fathers supported the subjugation of women in the Pauline and deutero-Pauline passages of scripture. Women were excluded from the official area of church life.

Canon law became very pronounced in deciding the fate of women. For example, Gratian, in his *Book of Decrees*, used the Pauline and deutero-Pauline passages to justify the slavish subjugation of women. The *Decretum Gratiani*, a collection of laws that superseded all older collections of laws up to the end of the twelfth century, prohibited women from exercising pastoral functions, as well as cultic and surgical practices. Pope Gregory XIII officially recognized it as the first part of the Corpus Iuris Canonici. The *Decretals* of Gregory IX supplemented the regulations for women contained in the *Decretum Griatiani*. It prohibited women from preaching, hearing confessions, or serving at the altar.[11]

Between the sixteenth and nineteenth centuries, different sentiments were expressed in the theological and canonistic literature to support or refute women's leadership roles in the church. Such literature included the views of Martin Luther who wrote to the Bohemian Brethren on the errors of the papal system. He upheld the Royal Priesthood concept in 1 Peter 2:9 as being universal and to be applied to every man, woman, and child in the body of Christ. He argued that women should be allowed to conduct baptism and communion services.[12] Yet the struggles of women for greater opportunities (in the church) continued into the seventeenth and succeeding centuries. Eventually, canon law recognized "active" congregations of women as being religious, but this sanction proved to be more theoretical than practical since theology and canon law was male oriented. As a result, women's position and status in the church remained stagnant. They were denied the opportunity for higher ecclesiastical studies and were either excluded from ministry altogether or assigned to inferior positions within the ministry. Women in leadership positions were treated with hostility and disdain, and their vacation was devalued and frowned upon. Elizabeth Carroll aptly pointed out that the tradition of exclusion of women from official ministry in the church was based on "a substructure of scriptural commentaries and canonical legislation" that men used to justify women's exclusion and that women used to internalize their inferiority.[13]

In reference to the Anglican Church, women are excluded in some parts of the world from participating in the ritual functions of the priest, including sacramental services. Elizabeth Canham recalled her marginalization in the Anglican Church in Britain due to her gender. In her book *Pilgrimage to Priesthood*, she described how the Anglican Church in England rejected her gift for ministry as a priest. She migrated to the United States of America in search of a parish. In Canada, some women in ministry feel excluded because they are not allowed to function as priests in some dioceses and are excluded from social conversations and certain official functions. Some have quit the ministry due to discouragement and marginalization in their workplaces.[14]

In his remarks on the present-day church, G. Curtis Jones stated that male chauvinism is most pronounced in the structure and leadership of the church. He commented on the slowness of the church to acknowledge the significant role of women in the expansion and enrichment of Christianity. He recognized that qualified women who enter the vacations of the church do not attempt to seek status or to rebel against the patriarchal protocol of the church, but do so as a "concrete illustration of the phenomenon of Christian compulsion, the indiscriminate call to serve." He clearly stated that God's selective service system is transcendent of traditions and sex and that servanthood and leadership involve humanity and genuineness, Christian faith and love versus human gender. He also recognized that some men and women may be faced with difficulties that may prevent them from functioning fully as ministers and alluded to integrated ministry in the church or to team ministry in the case of a husband and wife.[15]

Becker highlighted the root problems underlying the struggles of women leaders in ministry in a very succinct manner. She identified women as working in an alien environment in which they fight an uphill battle for job status and even for the opportunity to be effective leaders. Increasingly, women in various established denominations desire to enter the ordained or lay ministry in the church. However, even though some men and denominational policies may accept women in some ways, they still encounter several problems in working with men and in dealing with the hierarchy of denominations. Becker noted that large numbers of women have joined the ranks of church leaders but are forced to leave the church in large numbers as well. She described the ambivalence of men who are welcoming, optimistic, and appreciative of women, but who are also afraid, resentful, and confused in their treatment of women.[16]

The struggle of women for full acceptance by men in the church continues. The time must come for men and women to exist in unity in the church in exercising the spiritual gifts they are endowed with.

Perceived Sexist Discrimination against Women

Anderson and Clarke recorded many different forms of discrimination in the church in regard to women leaders in ministry based on a survey. They noted that men experience greater opportunities and have higher expectations than women who encounter more difficulty in ministry, especially in the beginning.

Traditional Roles

In the church, both male ministers and other people in the congregation attempt to slot women leaders into traditional roles such as working with children or young people.

Salary

Some women are discriminated against in terms of salary, or they encounter more difficulty than men to enter the most desired positions.

Single versus Married

Both married and single women encounter discrimination in different ways in ministry. In the case of a single person, the congregation may find it difficult to accept this person as a whole person. Some married women find it problematic to accept single women. Some denominations are reluctant to hire married women. Some women are kept on the fringes of ministry because their husbands are involved in ministry.[17] The author recalled a conversation with a female pastor who had founded her own "church" in 1999 and was subsequently married to a pastor in 2000. Her husband is now her copastor. Another male pastor referred to her as "the pastor's wife." This is a typical example of the inability of men everywhere to accept the stark reality of women leadership and a misconception that female leadership must automatically give way to male leadership, thus imposing on women secondary or marginalized roles and positions. As a result, some women with vibrant ministries are discriminated against based on gender and not necessarily on commitment, ability, or the calling of God on their lives.

Job Shortages

With the acceptance of women for ordination in many Protestant churches in America, the number of women enrolled in theological schools has soared in the United States of America, with women outnumbering men. However, the job search of women in ministry is hindered by the lack of full acceptance of female pastors by several congregations and the shortage of jobs. Male pastors are usually given preference for jobs as they are still considered the primary wage earners in North America. Women are forced to take to traditional fringe ministries such as family counseling, social service work, administrative fields, and special women ministries such as abortion counseling, family planning, ministry to battered wives, and ministry to prostitutes.[18]

Verbal and Sexual Harassment

Sexual harassment is a serious problem for women in ministry and is interdenominational. Anderson and Clarke noted that a great number of women whom they surveyed carried a severe burden of wounding encounters, most of which occurred behind closed doors, where women have been the victims of rude and disrespectful behaviors from their male counterparts. Some women reported verbal harassment while they were in seminary, which assumed the form of being wrongfully accused or of being unreasonably yelled at by their professors who felt threatened by them. They were penalized and made to cry in public. They also experienced unwelcome verbal behaviors by peers and very strong verbal harassment from some male students.

There was also a preponderance of information given by the sample of women to support pervasive sexual harassment of women in ministry. Such harassment varied from mild flirtation to sexual advances, which those women viewed as a source of annoyance rather than as a serious threat. Some of the flirtation began in the seminaries by some professors during the chaplaincy course or during their internship when their dressing was criticized, their knees were grabbed under the table, or their necks were touched. Some reported sexual harassment from male colleagues in ministry. Some minor forms of sexual harassment included being patted on the rump or being propositioned by strangers at clergy conferences with no active response from the denomination. A more serious form involved a pattern of sexual abuse of female students by a male staff at a retreat center, which culminated in the closure of that center after the students' exposure of the incident.[19] It was also noted that sexual harassment of female ministers was not only perpetrated by male ministers, but also by male members of some congregations.

Coping Strategies of Women Against Harassment

In order to cope with sexual discrimination and harassment in ministry, women have devised certain coping strategies that include challenging the perpetrators of sexual advance or ignoring them altogether. Some women may choose to leave their ministerial positions.

Since sexual harassment is perceived to be a widespread and deep-rooted problem that is confirmed to occur in various occupational categories and institutions, including the church,[20] women in ministry need to develop heightened awareness as to how to cope with this problem. Sexual harassment is a crime that courts severe penalties. It is a violation of the human rights legislation and should not be condoned. Anderson and Clarke felt that there is possibly a lack of preparedness among women to deal with this discrimination due to the idealism church women bring to their situation, including such ideals as acceptance, love, forgiveness, and open-mindedness. However, people in congregations are at different stages of their Christian growth, which results in different responses from different people to situations that arise in the church setting.[21] Despite this fact, women should exchange their long-standing ambivalence for affirmative action in dealing effectively with this problem in the church.

Three Phases of Marginalization

Despite the fact that women served with men as leaders within the early church setting prior to the institutionalization of the church, there are two main positions today among Evangelicals about women leaders in ministry. One position is put forward by the Egalitarians who believe that all areas of ministry should be open to women. They established their position from the historical examples of women leaders. The other position is put forward by the Complementarians who contend that women can appropriately serve in supported roles only. Their position stems from the view that men have traditionally exercised authority in the church, and they relegated that women leaders are to be confined to the fringes of Christian church life. They are satisfied with the relative absence of female church leaders.

Although male domination prevented female leadership in the church, Grenz and Kjesbo noted that women leaders continue to resurface due to their significant involvement in the renewal movements. Women lose significance when the movements become institutionalized, resulting in the infiltration of the church by a secular patriarchal structure that excludes women from leadership roles.[22]

Three phases of marginalization of women were noted in the religious movements beginning with the charismatic phase of the early days of the revival movements and culminating in the third phase of the bid for full institutional respectability.

During the first phase, women served as evangelists, church planters, and teachers. Records of the Moody Bible Institute confirm that there were women evangelists, Bible conference speakers, and Bible teachers lecturing to mixed audiences. This institute also supported the public ministry of women.

The second phase of marginalization was considered the credential phase in which leaders strove for respectability by becoming credential holders. Bible College education or seminary training and ordination were the initial prerequisites for ministry until it became increasingly difficult to acquire prerequisites to become credential holders.

The third phase stressed full institutional respectability when some participants of the movement strove for full acceptance by other prestigious denominations, most of which opposed female leadership. This opposition resulted in the exclusion of women from leadership roles.[23]

Issues of Invisibility and Silence

The invisibility and silence of women leaders have been no secret throughout the history of the church. Women have struggled for survival within the ranks of this institution as polarization between male and female leaders continues to exist. Women leaders have been suppressed and their very presence merely tolerated as though there was a conspiracy in the church to silence them. Yet the church continues to function with little recognition of their plight.

Hierarchy within the fabric of the church leaves women leaders with no other alternative than to be scattered everywhere. The church continues to function and act with female leadership being less significant than male leadership. Hence, women are denied ample space and a healthy environment to utilize their gifts, thus sacrificing their identity and development. They experience loneliness as "aliens" in a men's church and, because of marginalization, are crippled and unable to articulate their alienation. They struggle to be seen and heard.

As a marginalized group, women leaders continue to fight for survival in an unhealthy work environment in the church. They are faced with the onslaught of the "daily abuse of a system that does not fully recognize them." Musimbi Kanyoro cited "burn out" resulting from the inability of women leaders to take the daily abuse. Kanyoro also pointed out that some women might be forced to quit church work. Also, some women who are placed in leadership roles may be unable to support the participation of other women or may support a male style of leadership that is detrimental to them or to the organization.

Kanyoro noted that tokenism arises when there is a paucity of female representatives in an organization where these women cannot assume the burden of representing the possibilities of every woman in the organization. It was noted also that tokenism is detrimental to both marginalized groups and to their organizations, and often interesting changes do not take place until the number of women moves beyond the point of tokenism to about 20 percent or 30 percent of the institution.

In commenting on the backlash phenomenon, Kanyoro described it as a "reaction to policies which at some point are seen to promote justice, yet when they begin to make an impact, are questioned, especially by the dominant group in power." Men are recognized as the dominant group in the church's situation. Under this phenomenon, it is always beneficial for the dominant group, which feels that the system has betrayed it. Some notable results of backlashes are that men who might have previously supported women feel threatened and react in a negative manner. Also, some tasks may lose status as a result of becoming more female identified. Female decision makers may be assigned to departments with smaller budgets or less status. Also, women leaders may be set up for failure by being placed in decision-making positions in an organization that is crumbling and losing money and power.[24] These phenomena are also present in the church as an institution.

Subordinate Positions for Female Pastors in Relation to Male Pastors

In the church community, women usually hold subordinate positions. In most situations, women are at the lower rung of the hierarchy by serving as assistants to men in leadership positions even though some women are in the process of moving into positions that men formerly held in some churches. Women are concentrated at the assistant or associate levels of ministry or as Directors of Christian Education. They hold the less prestigious positions in the church, mainly working with women and children. They hold chaplaincy positions, which are usually open in some denominations, whether it is their first choice or not.[25]

The following accounts of a few female pastors paint a vivid picture of reality regarding some capacities in which women function in the church:

The Reverend Betty Ure recalled that in the mid-1940s, few women were allowed into the ministry. After she completed college, she had intended entering a seminary to work toward a Doctor of Religious Education degree since women were encouraged to pursue careers in this field. In the 1980s, approximately four decades later, this situation did not change drastically.[26]

The Reverend Betty Clark Moschella recalled in her affiliation with the Southern Baptists that even though a female pastor could be ordained, assume leadership roles, and pursue theological studies, it was another matter to be employed in ministry. She recalled that employment could take place if a woman was willing to work in fringe areas such as camp ministry, chaplaincy, religious education, or the ministry of music, none of which might have appealed to her. She recalled few openings for associate ministers that women could access and almost no positions for pastorates. She was advised that "the churches were not yet ready" to accept female pastors. Her advancement in ministry was painstakingly slow after she graduated from Harvard Divinity School in the 1980s. Although she was ordained in the Southern Baptist Church in Connecticut in 1983, she could not obtain employment in that denomination. She responded to an advertisement in the *Boston Globe* for a religious educator at Memorial Congregational Church in Massachusetts and became a half-time minister of Christian education. After one year, she became a three-quarter-time associate minister, then an interim minister after the senior pastor had retired.[27]

The ordination of women has not helped significantly in alleviating the disadvantaged situation female leaders are faced with. Female pastors experience several difficulties that may occur frequently in obtaining a first call and in experiencing resistance from lay persons. Their opportunities to move to higher positions within the church is hampered as they continue to be called to smaller and less secure congregations in some denominations. Even after parishioners accept them, they may still experience difficulty moving into senior pastorate positions.[28] As a result, women in the Baptist denomination are denied the opportunity of attaining positions of sole pastors or senior pastors. Denominations that ordain women should open more positions for women.[29]

Twentieth-Century Conferences and Movements to Address the Struggles

In an attempt to address the struggles of women leaders in ministry, several conferences and renewal movements addressed pertinent issues such as unity between men and women in the church and what it entails.

In 1927, the first conference on faith and order was held at Lausanne and was attended by six women and hundreds of men. These women raised the issue of the right place of women in the church and stressed the need for unity by examining the relationship of men and women. Then at the inauguration of the World Council of Churches in 1948, the first assembly resolved that "the church as the body of Christ consists of men and women created as responsible persons to glorify God and to do His will . . . . This truth, accepted in theory, is too often ignored in practice." This issue was subsequently placed on hold until the 1970s when a conference was held in Berlin between 1974 and 1975. Its assembly dealt with some pertinent issues. Firstly, it addressed "What Unity Requires" in regard to the women and men in the (faith) community as well as the wholeness of the body of Christ. The assembly concluded that "the unity of the church requires that women be free to live out their lives which God has given to them and to respond to their calling to share fully in the life and witness of the church." It saw the need to dwell on the issues of baptism, Eucharist, and ministry. The assembly also looked at "Structure of Injustice and Struggles for Liberation" and concluded that "the freedom and unity of Jesus Christ includes both halves of the human community; therefore it is imperative to the unity of the church and society that the full participation of women be given urgent consideration and immediate implementation."[30] The input from both of these conclusions bears testimony to the marginalization of women leaders in the church and to the struggles they have endured in search of greater freedom to use the gifts that God has entrusted to them fully. At present, this struggle continues.

---

1. Virgil Elizondo and Norbert Greinacher, eds., *Women in a Men's Church* (New York: The Seabury Press, 1980), 7–8, cited from Ida Ramming, "The Rise and Development of Male Domination."
2. Ibid., 8.
3. Ibid., 8–9, in *Didascalia et Constitutiones Apostolorum*, ed. F. X. Funk (Paperborn 1905) 1, 191, 199, 201; *Apostolische Konstitutionen* (Bibliothek der Kirchenväter 63, 1874), 115f, 120.
4. Kenneth and Alice Hamilton, *To Be a Man, to Be a Woman* (Nashville and New York: Abingdon Press, 1972), 152.
5. Dorothy R. Pape, *In Search of God's Ideal Woman: A Personal Examination of the New Testament* (Downers Grove, Illinois 60515: InterVarsity Press, 1977), 221.
6. Ibid., 222.
7. Elizondo and Greinacher, eds., op. cit., 3.
8. Ibid.
9. Pape, op. cit., 224.
10. Ibid., 225.
11. Elizondo and Greinacher, eds., op. cit., 10.
12. Pape, op. cit., 227.

13. Walter J. Burghardt, SJ, ed., *Woman: New Dimensions* (New York, Ramsey, Toronto: Paulist Press, 1977), 100–101, in Elizabeth Carroll, RSM, "Women and Ministry."
14. Grace M. Anderson and Juanne Nancarrow Clarke, *God Calls: Man Chooses: A Study of Women in Ministry* (Burlington, Ontario, Canada: Trinity Press, 1990), 114, cited from Elizabeth Canham, *Pilgrimage to Priesthood* (1982), 18.
15. G. Curtis Jones, *The Naked Shepherd: A Pastor Shares His Private Feelings about Living, Working and Growing Together in the Church* (USA: Word Books, 1979), 54–55.
16. Carol E. Becker, *Leading Women: How Church Women Can Avoid Leadership Traps and Negotiate the Gender Maze* (Nashville: Abingdon Press, 1996), 25–26.
17. Anderson and Clarke, op. cit., 111–115.
18. "We Listened Long Before We Spoke: Women theological students talk about theology, ministry, spirituality, vocation, mission, theological education and their dreams for the future of the church" (n.p., n.d.), 19–20.
19. Anderson and Clarke, op. cit., 112–118.
20. Ibid., 118–119.
21. Ibid., 112–113.
22. Stanley J. Grenz with Denise Muir Kjesbo, *Women in the Church: A Biblical Theology of Women in Ministry* (Downers Grove, Illinois: InterVarsity Press, 1995), 36–37.
23. Ibid., 37–38.
24. Musimbi Kanyoro, "Sitting Down Together," *Other Side* 34 (May–June 1998): 36–38.
25. Anderson and Clarke, op. cit., 18, 34.
26. The Bershire Clergywomen and Allison Stokes, *Women Pastors* (New York, New York 10017: The Crossroad Publishing Company, 1995), 31, The Reverend Betty Ure, "Where God Leads."
27. Ibid., 73–75; The Reverend Mary Clark Moschella, "Back Doors and Other Openings."
28. Becker, op. cit., 58.
29. Anderson and Clark, op. cit., 34.
30. Constance F. Parvey, ed., *The Community of Women and Men in the Church: A Report of the World Council of Churches' Conference Sheffield, England, 1981* (Geneva: World Council of Churches, 1983), 23–25, Phillip Potter, General Secretary, World Council of Churches, "A Chance to Change."

Chapter Seven:
Leadership Styles of Women

Styles of women leaders in ministry have brought to the church community new ways of leadership that are unique and special to female leaders. These new ways of leadership emerge from identifiable skills that these leaders bring to the ministry. In discussing the style of female leadership, Grenz and Kjesbo noted that women leaders stress "a collaborative, mutually facilitating and participative style of leadership," thus fostering a more egalitarian understanding of the church. They noted the contrast between this style of leadership and the hierarchical models that stress the distinctions between clergy and laity. Women promote a caring faith community, which emphasizes such feminine traits as compassion, mercy, and nurturance.[1] The traits and skills, which female leaders possess and embrace, seek to encourage more effective participation of the laity in ministry. Women leaders also encourage a more conducive atmosphere that fosters love.

Church Women and Their Style of Leadership

The style that women leaders bring to the ministry is one that they have created for themselves and one that differs from the leadership style of male leaders. It is very necessary for their style to be valued and validated for its true worth, without being labeled or identified as stereotypical. Becker noted that although women are aware of the differences between the leadership styles of men and women, women are very cautious of making certain claims and are reluctant to make a fixed distinction between the leadership styles of the sexes. Women are fearful that if they lay claim to certain differences in their leadership style, these differences can be used against them in the church. There is also the possibility that women's leadership style is determined by culture and enforced by the expectations of men and women. It is believed that women operate in styles that are more acceptable within existing paradigms.[2]

Although women work and function in a man's world, women leaders have less opportunities than men leaders to establish their authority and credibility. Yet there is need for women to be provided with these opportunities since their leadership may not be accepted in the same way as male leadership. Because of the hierarchical model of leadership that women have been conditioned to in the church, they are ambivalent about wielding powers as leaders and engaging in a collaborative form of leadership. It is not clear whether this collaborative form of leadership emerged because women are repulsed by the way the power of the hierarchical model has mitigated against them or whether they are truly collaborative leaders. For the last few generations, women have adhered to the male paradigm in the hierarchical model because they do not know another acceptable form of leadership. The room for the diversity of styles for women is limited. As a result, women are faced with the dilemma of successfully validating their style of leadership.

Collaborative leadership styles among women leaders include certain elements that go together for the successful implementation of their leadership style. Firstly, there is participatory management by which women elicit information and input from others prior to making decisions. Women leaders do not focus on wanting to be in control, but more importantly, on listening objectively to others in their decision-making process. Secondly, there is the willingness to share information. Women do not believe that they have all the answers or necessarily see themselves as experts. Their power is not derived from operating in a top-down position. The basis of the power is somewhere in the middle of concentric circles and is realized by the sharing of power, authority, and vision. By sharing power, women are empowered in leadership. Inextricably linked with their ability to collaborate is their ability to negotiate, which comes as a result of certain traits that women possess such as openness, sharing information, flexibility, and a commitment to resolve problems with people.

Because of their genuine concern for human relationships, women leaders are able to bring a more relational approach to their style of leadership. They show much care for people and their concerns. They nurture relationships and approach people on a relationship level that facilitates the willingness of others to execute the orders they give them. Women focus on building good relationships in their leadership. They regard caring for people and their concerns as crucial to getting the work done. This informal approach in relating to people breathes intimacy in the workplace, an intimacy that may make men uncomfortable.

Another skill which women possess is their ability to do many things simultaneously, which may have some bearing on their mothering experience. Women leaders are also not afraid to take risks even if their risk-taking involves deviating from what the male paradigm considers to be the norm. They see the possibility of others being influenced by their efforts and their views about what ministry should be like. They are able to break certain barriers as a result of their risk-taking.[3]

With the passage of time and the presence of more and more women in leadership, a new style of leadership between men and women has begun to emerge, referred to as "shared leadership" with a focus on partnership. However, women are still aware of the fact that they will never be accepted by men and that it is therefore necessary for them to be and remain unique. The need to remain unique stems from the fact that women are defined by a male standard.[4] They are striving to get a clear understanding of the styles of leadership they can safely exercise that are accepted by this standard. If they assume an authoritative goal-directed approach, they may be criticized for being unfeminine.

Paradigm of Woman Leadership

Because of the skills and attitudes they have developed from their shared experiences as women, women leaders are beginning to portray a new ministerial style. Donnelly referred to this style as being "Christ in the world, Christ present and active in receiving, healing, sustaining, guiding and reconciling." She viewed the realization of the self-giving of the Father and the Son through the Spirit as being integral to ministry as service. She believed that, from a position of helplessness as underdogs, women are in a better position than men to add deeper meaning to realizing the power of ministry, which is God's unconditioned love. Women are recipients of this love in a unique and special way and are able to share this love with others. For them, this experience assumes a different meaning.[5] It does not imply that men do not and cannot experience God's unconditioned love, but it does support the qualitative aspect of this experience for women.

Through their interactive style, women in both the secular and religious realms are able to share power and information. They are also able to enhance other people's self-worth and to get other people excited about what they are doing. They derive satisfaction from the connection they make and the process they use in realizing goals. Their authority and power are integral to their establishment of relationships. Because women are interested in competition, they bring a balance to their workplace as consensus managers. Through collaboration, they share their power with others to get the job done. Women do not focus on accumulating power on top but desire to see their power multiplied and shared with others. On the contrary, men act powerfully to influence others. Becker contended that women in leadership are an indication of women's search for an alternative way of ordering their reality and world, not simply of reversing the paradigm of domination.[6]

Zikmund, Lummis, and Chang interviewed 250 male and female pastors from fifteen denominations on telephone regarding women clergy's approach to ministry. Their survey revealed that many clergy believed that women clergy care more about the lives of individual members of their congregation, are more sensitive and nurturing, and more likely to use their personal experiences in preaching, teaching, and counseling than men. Women clergy are less interested in congregational politics, power over others, and job prestige. They are more relational than clergymen. They make decisions cooperatively rather than in a hierarchical or authoritative manner.

Here are some views of some clergywomen in different denominations. A Wesleyan clergywoman stated that the women leaders in her denomination employed a less hierarchical and more cooperative style. These leaders regarded themselves as empowering the laity rather than being its leaders. A Unitarian Universalist clergywoman said that in her denomination, women leaders tended to use more of a partnership style rather than a hierarchical leadership style. A United Church of Christ clergywoman felt that women had a different focus and style. They worked with the laity and were more interested in sharing power. In regard to the United Methodist clergywomen, the majority of them felt that women leaders shared power in leadership more than clergymen. It was also discovered that clergymen tended to work in a hierarchical system, from top to bottom. Clergywomen performed in concentric circles and attempted to involve the laity equally in decision making. Episcopal clergywomen had a vision for more inclusiveness. They employed participatory leadership techniques. American Baptist clergywomen were more able to empower people and work with them than their male counterparts but found it more difficult to exercise authority.[7]

Both the Reverend Allison Stokes and the Reverend Mary Clark Moschella gave a vivid glimpse of the female style of leadership as they recalled their involvement in ministry. Reverend Moschella felt that she was greatly supported by her pastoral relations committee that assisted her to focus on her goals and encouraged her in her attempt to change her administrative style. As a result, she was able to "claim the power of the pastoral role." Initially, she had been minimizing the power by trying to build a consensus and honoring everyone else's opinion until she discovered that she was called to lead by being more loyal to her own insights and instincts without ignoring other people's opinion. She expressed great affection for the people of Lee who showed her great respect.[8]

Reverend Stokes spoke of assuming a style of leadership that was collaborative and not hierarchical. She aspired to lead by consensus building. She strove to empower her congregation on one hand and, on the other hand, to disempower those who wished to "dominate, control or manipulate all decision-making within the church." Although there were conflicts in her congregation, with the help of three moderators, she was able to deal with these differences successfully through a spirit of cooperation and fellowship.[9]

Locus of Leadership Power

Parvey identified some models of leadership that are favorable to women. Firstly, there is *the leader from below* model whose aim is to serve the needs of the community. It has an integrative or holistic approach and includes rational decision. Secondly, there is the model of *teamwork at the top of the hierarchy of organizations*. Its leadership is equal, and teamwork is practiced in all layers of the organization. Its goals are to share information and decision making, to promote everyone's personality, and to permit complementary use of gifts and participation. Thirdly, there is the model of *nonhierarchical leadership* that has a small core team that serves as a resource to the remainder of the leadership circle. Many people will acquire skill in exercising leadership due to limited terms of office.[10]

Partnership Style and Stress in Leadership

In her examination of the factor of stress in relation to the pastor's leadership style and the congregation's leadership style expectations, Coger relied on a research that was done by Roy Oswald in the *The Pastor as Newcomer* where he surmised that "congregations seem to develop a corporate expectation for the kind of leadership they want from a pastor. Should the new pastor's leadership style differ significantly from this expectation, conflict can be expected."[11] He viewed leadership style in light of a low to high range of pastor initiative and a low to high range of congregational initiative.

As a disadvantaged, marginalized group, women leaders may experience intensified stress when they are working in a congregation that devalues or sabotages their contribution. Several women leaders described their ideal style of ministry as "partnership, working with, enabling, and equipping the saints, co-workers and co-laborers." However, these leaders were exposed to severe stress when their congregations failed to respond by actively participating in getting the job done. Conflict and stress could have been reduced significantly when these leaders experienced mutual ministry in their congregations.[12]

Coger has identified two factors that can assist in fostering the partnership style. One of these factors is the congregation's willingness to assume responsibility for decision making and program implementation. The second factor is the issue of authority that is derived from a mutual understanding between laity and clergy of the tasks to be performed and clarity of expectations for working together.[13] The presence of these two elements is the key for the success of the partnership style.

In their performance of leadership roles, women employ the principles discussed in this chapter. In their quest to establish a paradigm for their leadership style, women have been able to use these principles in their leadership effectively. However, these principles are not necessarily endorsed by men and may be opposed by some women, resulting in the lack of recognition of this leadership style as an integral and valid part of what may be considered effective leadership. There is dire need for women to support effective female leadership and to continue sharing their experiences. Women envision the dream of establishing an empowering leadership style that involves collaboration, egalitarianism, and empowerment that will one day truly become a recognized component of effective leadership in the church community. Although women may be unable to change the existing structures and institutions of the church, it is imperative for their leadership style to be recognized and validated as something truly unique.

---

1. Stanley J. Grenz with Denise Muir Kjesbo, *Women in the Church: A Biblical Theology of Women in Ministry* (Downers Grove, Illinois: InterVarsity Press, 1995), 25–26
2. Carol E. Becker, *Leading Women: How the Church Can Avoid Leadership Traps and Negotiate the Gender Maze* (Nashville: Abingdon Press, 1996), 42–44.
3. Ibid., 38–42.
4. Ibid., 43–45.
5. Clare Benedicks Fischer, Betsy Brenneman, and Anne McGrew Bennett, eds., *Women in a Strange Land: Search for a New Image* (Philadelphia: Fortress press, 1975), 94–96; Dorothy Donnelly, CSJ, "The Gifted Woman: New Style for Ministry."
6. Becker, op. cit., 52–53.
7. Barbara Brown Zikmund, Adair T. Lummis, and Patricia M. Y. Chang, "Women, Men and Styles of Clergy Leadership" [Online] Available wysiwyg//35/http://hirrhartaem.edu/bookshelf/clergywomen_summary.html, 1–3.
8. The Berkshire Clergywomen and Allison Stokes, *Women Pastors* (New York, New York 10017: The Crossroad Publishing Company, 1995), 79, the Reverend Mary Clark Moschella, "Back Doors and Other Openings."
9. Ibid., 45; Allison Stokes, "Being a Pastor/Scholar: A Calling within a Calling."
10. Constance F. Parvey, ed., *The Community of Women and Men in the Church: A Report of the World Council of Churches' Conference Sheffield, England, 1991* (Geneva: World Council of Churches, 1983),136–137.
11. Marian Coger, *Women in Parish Ministry: Stress & Support* (The Alban Institute, 1991), 10, Roy M. Oswald, *The Pastor as Newcomer* (The Alban Institute, 1977). 11.
12. Ibid., 11.
13. Ibid., 11–12.

Conclusion:
Beyond the Present— A New Approach to Ministry

There is a rich heritage of women leaders in ministry etched in the annals of church history despite women's history of subordination and inferior status in society and the various theories and schools of thought that discredit or limit a woman's use of authority and power. Despite man-made limitations placed upon women in the exercising of spiritual gifts and in their performance of roles and functions in the organizational component of the church, women leaders in ministry continue to be a formidable force to be reckoned with in Christendom. Women will not be denied, nor will those who have the call of God on their lives and are empowered by the Holy Spirit be silenced. The time has come to break the shackles that bind many gallant women of God to the church as an organization and to focus on the true place of women in the charismatic or spiritual component of the church. This is the most significant part of the church, the body of Christ. The time has come for ministry as it pertains to both men and women to be viewed as vibrant and active service, which is all-inclusive and tailored to accommodate both male and female. With this in mind, a new approach to ministry seems inevitable.

Charismatic and Administrative Components of the Church

Conflict has arisen in the church because of lack of clarity between the charismatic and administrative components of the church: the overshadowing of the charismatic component by the administrative component and man's inclination to place more emphasis on the administrative component. In order to examine issues surrounding a new approach to ministry, it is necessary to get a better understanding of how these two components of the church operate. William R. Cunningham noted that in the history of the church, the spiritual component was first established and is considered the foundation of the true church, the body of Christ. The Holy Spirit joins people together to form the body and is the leader of the church with Jesus Christ as its head.

In the charismatic component of the church, there are no scriptural restrictions placed on women in ministry. Any restrictions placed on women in ministry are culturally biased and man-made. Cunningham stated that any restrictions placed on women in church service are organizational and not Christian restrictions. He argued that discriminations against women did not originate from the Christian faith that promotes the idea of equality in terms of rights and privileges. The fivefold ministry of pastor, teacher, prophet, evangelist, and apostle comprises this component. Initially, these were regarded as ministries and not offices or positions.

The man-made administrative component of the church arose to give structure to and to maintain organization in an ever-growing body. As a result, church offices were created. Elders, bishops, and deacons made up this component. The office of Elders, the original leaders of the local churches, was reserved for men due to the customs and culture in those days. Women were excluded from leadership even though they played a significant role in the charismatic component of the church. Only men served as administrative officials.[1] Men who are yoked in tradition need the scales to fall from their eyes so that their spiritual understanding may be illumined. The war between the charismatic and administrative components of the church that results in utter chaos must cease so that the church can be united.

Servanthood in Ministry

The concept of servanthood in ministry is bound up with the charismatic component of the church. Christians are called to servanthood, which does not signify oppression, subordination, or inferiority. Christians are servants, elected by God for service.

Jesus Christ was the epitome of a servant and servanthood. He was portrayed as a suffering servant in Isaiah and, in the New Testament, as the bringer of the new age of deliverance and liberation (Isaiah 53;

Matthew 12:15–21; Acts 3:13). As a servant, He offered Himself freely and accepted service and love in return (Philippians 2:7; Luke 7: 32–50, 6:1–11, 10:38–42).

In the early church, the Apostles were also called to serve in the witness of the Gospel. The Apostle Paul considered himself a slave of Christ by his participation in God's liberating action with Christ (1 Corinthians 9:19). Reference was made in the New Testament to women as servants and apostles. Today, God is still calling both men and women in the church to the privileged role of servants and apostles in service for God.

There is need today for a reciprocal relationship and service that is shared by both male and female leaders in ministry. Men and women must develop new ways of cooperating as God's servants in His service. This relationship for service should be modeled after the lifestyle of Jesus Christ, one in which women leaders are liberated to serve and be served without experiencing the loss of their identity or fear of subordination. Men and women are to unite as partners in recognizing the beauty and power in servanthood.[2]

Peter Selby, in his defense of women pastors, clamored for a just relationship between women and men, grounded in God's free generosity. Such a relationship will be realized when women are included in all spheres of ministry and not merely (in) rearranging some of the external symbols of status and continuing to perpetuate a baleful division of labor. The pastoral and other talents of women cannot be honored in this fashion. Selby supported the inclusion of women as equal partners with men in Christian ministry since they are able to offer rich resources of mutual nourishment and care. He felt that by admitting them as priests and bishops in the church's ministry, injustice would be removed. He called for a relationship between woman and man that reflects and moulds the way in which God's nature and relationship to us are understood and saw the "rights" of women as grounded in God's unconstrained freedom to call and bless whom He chooses.[3] However, this injustice is so entrenched in the structure of the church that to remove it will require close scrutiny of every area of church life, of prevailing attitudes of decision-making bodies and officials in the church, of the attitudes and expectations of the laity, and of past and present cultures that have placed women in subordinate roles and devalued their status. Although achievable, this task is huge and insurmountable.

In his introductory essay on *The New Relatedness for Man and Woman in Christ*, James B. Torrance referred to the Trinitarian understanding of male-female relations. He reported Dr. Olsen as pleading with us to recover this understanding of male-female relations, which can be interpreted in terms of our union with God in Christ in terms of caring love and mutual functional complementarity and mutual submission. Although men and women are sexually diverse, because there is neither male nor female in Christ, man and woman find the fulfillment of their maleness and femaleness in Christ in equality, unity, mutuality, and complementarity.[4]

God created male and female in His image, resulting in a male-female oneness and equality and cooperative and mutual interdependence. When God created Eve from Adam's rib, she was created to be Adam's partner. In turn, Adam found wholeness in complementary fellowship with Eve. The wholeness of personhood is derived from man-male and man-female that coexist. Man and woman complement each other in service within the framework of love.[5]

Effects of the Fall on Man and Woman Relationships

In creation, God created man and woman to live in harmonious fellowship with him and with each other. Man and woman were created equal and complementary to each other. Subordination was absent in the male-female relation. As self-conscious moral beings, Adam and Eve enjoyed freedom in their relationship with God. However, after man sinned through disobedience, the result was a broken relationship between God and man and between man and man. Hence, the relationship, which was established between Adam and Eve at creation, became distorted. The union they experienced in marriage was broken, and marriage became an institution with the development of man-made laws to govern it. The harmonious and intimate relationship, which they once shared, became conflicting and corrupt, thus deviating from the original intent of the marriage relationship. God pronounced judgment on man, which not only emphasized that by sinning, Adam and Eve had transgressed by deliberately distorting realities that already existed, but also defined a new life situation within the framework of the fall.

As a result, man was to rule over woman, symbolic of subordination on one hand (Genesis 37:8; Exodus 21:8; Deuteronomy 15:6; Joel 2:17), but also protection and caring on the other hand (Genesis 1:16). The destructive power of death and enmity became real to man (Genesis 3:15–19). Man became his own enemy, with the symbolic use of the sword with power and authority over the subordinate. The practice of the male-dominated society emerged, resulting in patriarchal dominance, polygamy, concubines, and double standards of adultery and divorce. Another result of the fall was that distinctive roles for man and woman became flawed and painful. Originally, God's command to Adam and Eve to "be fruitful and multiply" was a pleasant and delightful experience. This experience was to change to an onerous and burdensome one after the fall.[6] Woman was now to bring forth children in physical pain and sorrow. The spiritual separation of man and woman from God adversely affected their entire life. Therefore, woman was now faced with sorrow to bring forth children, to nurture, and to raise them. On the other hand, man was to become the breadwinner of his family and to toil for his living. Man and woman were to suffer physical death because of their act of disobedience in eating the forbidden fruit.

Impact of the Effects of the Fall on the New Creation

The crux of ordering in the church, which mitigates against the full participation of women leaders in the church, lies in the subordination theory, which supports the view that man was created to be the leader and woman to be his subordinate. It is a given fact that man's rulership over woman is interwoven in the fabric of society and is present in the hierarchical structure of the church. Did God predestine His church to function in this fashion?

When analyzing the church in light of the New Creation theory, Grenz and Kjesbo noted that God's ultimate goal of human history is to establish community in the highest sense. In the church, God's goal sets the context for the biblical understanding of the church as His intention is to forge a reconciled people who reflect the character of their Creator and Redeemer. The church community should live according to the vision of the New Creation that anticipates a day of complete reconciliation among God's people. The New Creation consists of the renewal and completion of creation. The vision of God's future community should be reflected in the appearance of the present corporate life of God's people,[7] void of any hierarchical structures that reflect human distinctions in the church for centuries. This corporate life must involve the presence and participation of women and men in the church. In preparation for God's eschatological reign when perfect fellowship between God and man will become reality, Grenz and Kjesbo saw the call for full participation of man and woman in the church as the fulfillment of God's egalitarian intention from the dawn of creation.[8]

The vision of God's plan for His new creation began to take shape and form with the advent of Christ, when God's intention for man and creation unfolded. The effects of the fall, which previously dominated human living, were superseded by a new structure of interpersonal relationship. Because gender-based discrimination opposes the biblical vision of God's intention for creation, Christ's redemptive work has liberated us from the role of hierarchy as the fundamental principle for male-female relationships. As a result, gender-based discrimination should not be the criterion for determining responsibilities within a fellowship. This view is substantiated by Peter's declaration of man and woman as coheirs of the gift of salvation (1 Peter 3:7) and Paul's statement about the oneness of male and female in Jesus Christ (Galatians 3:28) referred to elsewhere as the Magna Carta of Christianity.[9]

This oneness of male and female in Christ refers strictly to equality in salvation. Spiritually, male and female are equal. Olsen stressed that this oneness and equality do not mean sameness, but exist in interdependence where a man and a woman remain male and female. The words *male* and *female* connote gender differentiation, an essential quality of man and woman from birth that cannot be altered. He also emphasized that male-female relationship is to be an image of the triune God. Male and female must imitate the principle of divine relatedness expressed in oneness, equality, and functional complementarity.[10]

A Reflection on Early Christianity

Early Christian communities mirrored a kind of community that appeared to be more in keeping with the divine human community that God has called His church to form. This community should be marked by mutuality and partnership. It should be one in which an individual's dignity is respected and where the complementarity of gifts is in operation. The early church communities emphasized solidarity and sharing, which transcended traditional status boundaries of sex, class, and culture. A new way of life emerged, which included sharing of property, table fellowship, slaves, women, and outcasts. The poor were attended to. A new family of brothers and sisters in Christ superseded the patriarchal family of the society and the church.[11]

In the days of Jesus Christ, His attitude toward women was accepting and deviated from the cultural norms that endorsed male domination over female. He treated women with the same dignity as men and viewed their abilities on par with their male counterparts. Under His ministry, there were female disciples and apostles who participated in His ministry and attended to His physical needs, who followed as witnesses to His death on the cross, and to whom He entrusted the responsibility to proclaim His resurrection.

The Apostle Paul patterned his ministry after some basic tenets that Jesus Christ upheld. Some of his most active and significant helpers or partners in ministry were women aforementioned in chapter 3. Under His ministry, women served as both leaders and coleaders of house churches. Women who were married like Priscilla ministered with their husbands in mutual partnership, which was a significant and healthy development in the life and effectiveness of the early church. This development was the epitome of the baptismal formula put forward by Paul in Galatians 3:21–28 where all human beings who are baptized into Christ have put on Christ and where any distinction based on status, race, or sex is eliminated.

Just when the church appeared to be headed in the right direction for the fulfillment of God's plan for the redeemed, the foundations of the church were shaken and altered for centuries by the evolution of man-made structures for its governance. The earliest Christian communities had experienced and had thrived on less structure. They were governed by the authority of the Apostles and by the experience of the Spirit and the exercising of the gifts in the church community. However, these were subsequently replaced by a more structured church order that fostered the exercising of the authority in a hierarchical manner. In this hierarchical structure, a wide chasm was created between the laity and the clergy, and an all-male hierarchy,[12] which hindered the full participation of women in ministry, controlled the ministers.

The Church as a Liberation Community

The church is a Christian community that was established in unity with Christ as its head. It is Jesus Christ, through the Holy Spirit, who unites the family of faith in the church community. The members of this community should focus on crippling the constraints of patriarchy and the social structures that hinder this system of church order. This community should foster and nurture liberating ways in male-female relationship and a transformation of leadership in ministry by promoting women pastors and shared ministry.

In the Section Reports on *Identity and Relationships in the New Community*, participants of the World Council of Churches envisioned this new, liberating community as one that is unified and is striving to express itself as the body of Christ. Its value will be loving relationships, and its basis, love that encompasses respect for all persons. It will respect differences and diversities, find fulfillment in sharing and partnership, and serve as an inexhaustible source of mutual enrichment and growth. It will support, enable, and affirm people's development and provide them with a creative, dynamic environment in which to experience life.[13]

In order for the new community to mature and bear fruit, women must remain autonomous human beings. Both men and women have entertained the wishful thinking that the church is functioning as a loving family, with a great cause in which self is forgotten. Now men and women must separately accept the pain of division, which both of them may find very difficult. Women may find it difficult because they are accustomed to performing secondary roles, and men, because of their patriarchy of love engendered by their official ranks and power in the church. Love must not be viewed in terms of smothering but must be viewed as one in which no domination is perpetrated.

The emancipation of women from historical subjection will result in men having to undergo the painful process of relearning as they become insecure in the masculine roles that have been instilled in them. More significantly, manly pride will be violated and man's self-respect shaken. Man's identity with patriarchy will crumble. On the other hand, women will experience a new identity that will catapult them into complete humanity. Women will experience an explosion of previously pent-up creativity. In order for the emancipation of women to succeed, men must be freed simultaneously from patriarchy. Man must discover the good of relationship, fellowship, and community. He must develop a heightened awareness and understanding of the core of human nature and abandon self-righteousness in preparation for honest friendship and brotherhood. Man must stop identifying with the male caste and break away from the male code. He must be willing to abandon the masculine privileges conferred on him through patriarchy and abandon or limit his male responsibility toward the weaker sex.[14]

Ministry as Mutual Empowerment of the New Community

In order to experience ministry in its real form of service, Ruether felt clericalism, which disempowers people by making them dependent on the clergy and which fosters leadership that reduces others to subjects to be governed, should be dismantled. Under clericalism, there is the assumption that people have no direct access to God since the clergy serves as mediator between God and man. The clergy possesses certain rights and privileges such as authorized theological training, authority to preach, teach, and admonish the church, and sacramental powers.

Ministry transfers leadership, which exerts power over others, to one that empowers others and generates relations of mutual empowerment. Ruether believed that in ministry, power should be exercised to liberate people. This liberation can be realized by allowing people with different gifts to experience empowerment (by way of) exercising these gifts in the community and by affording each person the confidence and skills to develop these gifts for the ministry. All of these gifts are unique and essential to liberate a church and must blend with one another to realize a community that reflects and acts on the gospel of liberation.

Ruether further believed that people should be empowered collectively to administer the sacraments, such as the Eucharist and Baptism, which express the redemptive life of the church. She did not subscribe to the notion that the administering of the sacraments should be done by a person who is set apart in specialized ministry. In this regard, she believed that the members of the community could develop the skill, expertise, and empowerment to minister.[15]

The Future of Women in Ministry

In order to envision a good and positive prognosis for the future of women in ministry, the situation that existed in the early church should be revisited. In the days of Jesus Christ and Paul, the church afforded women the opportunity to assume leadership roles, which lasted for many centuries up to the Renaissance period. Since then, patriarchy reasserted itself in the church community and continues to be the order of the day. The future of women leaders in ministry weighs in the balance with a deformed church that is grounded in Judeo-Greco-Roman biases of patriarchy. There is dire need for equality in the ministry of the church where the cultural biases of race, ethnicity, social standing, and gender will be eliminated and where women will be able to use their reasoning and intellectual powers in serving God and the church.[16]

While women continue to support the church, McClung stated that sex prejudice, which is hard to break down, will continue. She noted that the smaller a man is, the narrower is his soul and the stronger he will cling to his belief in his own superiority. She commended the best and ablest men who have taken up the cause of women for their brotherly companionship and fair-mindedness. She commented on the valuable assistance that women have provided men in the church as helpmates to achieve success and stressed the ineffectiveness of the church in failing to use one wing of its army. Men have been in control for too long to test their abilities as arbiters of human destiny. Some people who are high in authority in the church have argued that the admission of women to every department in the church will create the tendency to drive out men. The small attendance of men at church is blamed by some on "the feminization of the church," which can be viewed as an example of women being held in mild contempt.[17]

Solution of Women Leaders' Problem

The struggles of women to liberate themselves from the shackles of patriarchy, oppression, discrimination, marginalization, and subjugation within the confines of the church have been long and hard. As a structural organization, the church has proven to be a formidable force behind whose shroud the walls of partition between man and woman dangle, and the venom of segregation lurks. The church has failed to serve as a bastion of liberation where male and female leaders can labor together in harmony for the propagation of the Gospel of Christ and for the exercising of spiritual gifts, which the Holy Spirit has endowed them with. The time has come for the cloak under which male domination and supremacy have been sheltered to be removed. There is a need for a new beginning in the church and for a total overhaul of the structural component of the church to successfully coexist and blend with its charismatic component in order to ensure a bright future in the church community for women leaders.

In an effort to resolve the problems of women leaders in ministry, the evolving structure of the church must be scrutinized to determine whether the forms that currently exist are up-to-date for fulfilling the needs of the present-day church or whether they are antiquated or whether they have kept abreast with the changing times and with the struggles of women to be seen and heard. Certainly, there is evidence within the existing structures of the church of injustices that need to be addressed before any significant progress in the operation of the church can be realized.

Firstly, the church must move away from patriarchy, which it fostered for centuries. Patriarchy is an antiquated cultural form that dates back to hundreds of years. Although it has served its purpose in influencing certain cultural, economic, and religious arenas the world over, it has now proven to be a gigantic hindrance in the progress of the church and in the cause of women leaders in ministry. It is an ancient system of male domination, which did not originate with Christianity, but was embraced by the church. This system served in the church to oppress, silence, and cripple women. Women are now seeking freedom from the cruel grasp of patriarchy to experience a new community where those without power are listened to by those with power, where the powerless is mobilized to get organized, where justice prevails by the redistribution of power or by the relinquishing of power by those with power.[18] Indeed, patriarchy, which has a crippling influence on the liberation of religious practices in the church, should be eradicated from the church community.

Secondly, a reconstruction of religious practices to reflect egalitarianism is of paramount importance if the human rights of women leaders are to be honored and respected within the church. In its absence, the basic needs of women leaders are subjugated to the needs of male leaders. Egalitarianism results in religious institutions and authorities that propagate gender inequality being scrutinized and exposed. It undermines the patriarchal family structure in which females and their sexuality are in subjugation to the male head of the household. The values of the patriarchal structure merged with religious institutions to become the root problem in the mutual recognition of the full humanity of all members of the family and of the church. Scovill noted that many different techniques are needed to free the egalitarian core of the religious tradition from nonegalitarian cultural accretions in pursuit of gender equality. Such techniques include a basic knowledge and study of religious texts and traditions that would hold religious leaders and adherents accountable to the egalitarian core of tradition, the study of traditions to unearth past egalitarian traditions, a close examination of rituals and traditions initiated by women for empowering them in the social sphere and for affirming their innate ability to connect with ultimate reality, and the reconstruction and reformulation of religious practices and traditions to align them with the egalitarian vision at the center of religious tradition.[19]

Thirdly, there is need for the reordering of the church. Initially, the church order was rooted in the tradition of Jesus Christ and was created by the church to address its needs in an attempt to live out the mission and ministry of Jesus Christ. Equality and mutuality were present in the exercising of the ministerial gifts. However, over the centuries, a clear line of demarcation between the clergy and the laity emerged, resulting in an impoverished church and a passive and powerless laity. For the most part, ministerial gifts lay dormant and undeveloped. Even gifted women, as part of the laity, were prohibited from exercising their gifts in mutual partnership in the ministry and were barred from functioning publicly and officially in the promulgation of the Gospel. This function was monopolized by male celibate clerics.[20] This structure has already served its purpose and has now become obsolete in terms of where the institutional church is in its stage of development. The existence of a hierarchical superior priestly caste may be considered outdated as the emphasis is shifted from the priest, who is regarded as one who exclusively offers sacrifice, to one who performs a ministerial role, which removes the priest from his position as overseer, and puts him in close contact with the world. It presents him as a brother rather than as a father. The priest is now viewed in terms of mission to the world, which requires him to dialogue and cooperate with his fellowmen.[21]

Because in present-day society, new needs, cultural experiences and awareness, and actual knowledge of cultural differentiations have emerged, there is a heightened awareness that desired changes must take place in the church order to make its service more relevant to contemporary society. Brennan stressed the importance of the laity, including women, to participate actively in the reconstruction of the church order. In this reconstruction, much emphasis should be placed on democratization of the male-female relations. New models of community and lifestyle and of partnership should emerge within the church to break down the walls of segregation between the sexes and between the clergy and laity. The laity should be given greater responsibility and full recognition that is commensurate with cultural awareness. Some competent professional laymen may be more specialized to perform work in different fields and areas than members of the clergy and should be given the opportunity to perform such tasks, in ways of recognizing and using the gifts and talents of the gifted. Most importantly, women should play a very significant role in the reconstruction of the church order. Some women are also included among the gifted. Women should be allowed to fully participate in the church community that emphasizes the charismatic component of the body of Christ, which encompasses partnership in the ministry and the complementarity of gifts in the execution of the mission and ministry of Jesus Christ. Gifts that women are endowed with should be fully recognized and endorsed as being entrusted to them by the Holy Spirit.[22]

Women leaders should not be held at bay and treated as subordinates to their male counterparts in terms of their roles, functions, and status in the ministry. They should not be expected to serve in fringe areas of ministry only or be excluded from certain areas of ministry. They should not be made to feel as aliens and misfits in an institution that depersonalizes and destroys the Christian spirit of ministry. Indeed, the church must promote cooperation among its people and an atmosphere of trust in which the ministries of women leaders can flourish and become legitimized. Women should play an integral part in goal-setting and in the decision-making process of the church. As heirs, heirs of God and joint heirs with Christ, and as part of the royal priesthood, women are equal representatives of Christ to the world, equal partners with male leaders in Christ's church. While freedom reigns in the hearts and lives of women leaders and as they march forward as soldiers of the cross and as champions in ministry, let their full acceptance and participation in ministry prevail!

---

1. William R. Cunningham, "A Scriptural Perspective on the Place of Women," © 2000, Second Edition [Online] Available http://www.pursuingthetruth.org/studies/files/placeofwomen.htm, February 7, 2001.
2. Alice Hageman in collaboration with the Women's Caucus of Harvard Divinity School, *Sexist Religion and Women in the Church: No More Silence!* (New York: Association Press, 1974), 54–58, in Letty M. Russell, "Women and Ministry."
3. Richard Hollaway, ed., *Who Needs Feminism? Male Responses to Sexism in the Church* (Great Britain: SPCK, 1991), 130–133; in Peter Selby, "They make such good Pastors."
4. V. Norskov Olsen, *The New Relatedness for Man & Woman in Christ: A Mirror of the Divine* (Loma Linda,California: Loma Linda University. Center for Christian Bioethics, 1993), 16–20, in James B. Torrance, "Introductory Essay."
5. Ibid., 44–52.
6. Ibid., 34–57.
7. Stanley J. Grenz with Denise Muir Kjesbo, *Women in the Church: A Biblical Theology of Women in Ministry* (Downers Grove, Illinois: InterVarsity Press, 1995), 174–179.
8. Ibid., 179.
9. Ibid., 176–177.
10. Olsen, op. cit., 102–103.
11. Lisa Sowle Cahill, *Sex, Gender, and Christian Ethics* (Great Britain: Cambridge University Press, 1996), 150.
12. Virgil Elizondo and Norbert Greinacher, eds., *Women in a Men's Church* (New York: The Seabury Press, 1980), 103–108, in Margaret Brennan, "Women and Men in Church Office."

13. Constance F. Parvey, ed., *The Community of Men and Women in the Church: A Report of the World Council of Churches' Conference Sheffield, England, 1981* (Geneva: World Council of Churches, 1983), 109–110.
14. Ibid., 38–39, in Elisabeth Moltmann-Wendel and Jürgen Moltmann, "Becoming Human in New Community."
15. Rosemary Radford Ruether, *Sexism and God Talk: Toward a Feminist Theology* (Boston: Beacon Press, 1983), 206–209.
16. Grace M. Anderson and Juanne Nancarrow Clarke, *God Calls: Man Chooses, A Study of Women in Ministry* (Burlington, Ontario. Canada: Trinity Press, 1990), 44.
17. Nellie L. McClung, *In Times Like These* (Toronto and Buffalo: University of Toronto Press, 1972), 70–75.
18. Parvey, op. cit., 30–31, in Elisabeth Moltmann-Wendel and Jürgen Moltmann, op. cit.
19. Nelia Beth Scovill, "The Liberation of Women: Religious Sources" [Online] Available http://www.consultation.org/consultation/libpub.htm, 22/04/2001, 2.
20. Elizondo and Greinacher, eds., op. cit., 106, in Margaret Brennan, "Women and Men in Church Office."
21. Mary Daly, *The Church and the Second Sex* (Boston: Beacon Press, 1985), 207.
22. Elizondo and Greinacher, eds., op. cit., 107–108.

Bibliography

Books

_____ ed. *Women in the World's Religions : Past and Present.* New York: Paragon House, 1987.

_____ . *Sex, Gender and Christian Ethics.* Great Britain: University Press Cambridge, 1996.

_____. *The Church and the Second Sex.* Boston: Beacon Press, 1985.

Ajibola, Faith B. *The Galilean Women of Today.* Ibadan: Feyisetan Press, 1998.

Anderson, Grace M. and Juanne Nancarrow Clarke, *God Calls: Man Chooses – A Study of Women in Ministry.* Burlington, Ontario, Canada: Trinity Press, 1990.

Becker, Carol E. *Leading Women: How Church Women Can Avoid Leadership Traps and Negotiate the Gender Maze,* Nashville: Abingdon Press, 1996.

Byrne, Lavinia. *Women Before God: Our Own Spirituality.* Connecticut: Mystic, Twenty-Third Publications, 1988.

Bristow, John Temple. *What Paul Really Said about Women – An Apostle's Liberating Views on Equality in Marriage, Leadership and Love.* San Francisco: Harper, 1991.

Buhrig, Marca. *Woman Invisible: A Personal Odyssey in Christian Feminism.* Turnbridge Wells, Kent: Burns & Oates, 1993.

Burghardt, SJ and J. Walter, ed. *Woman New Dimensions.* New York, Ramsey, Toronto: Paulist Press, 1977.

Cahill, Lisa Sowle. *Between the Sexes: Foundation for a Christian Ethics of Sexuality.* Philadelphia: Fortress Press, 1985.

Clark, Elizabeth A., and Herbert Richardson, eds. *Women and Religion: The Original Sourcebook of Women in Christian Thought.* San Francisco: Harper, 1996.

Clouse, Bonnidell and Robert G. Clouse, eds. *Women in Ministry: Four Views.* Downers Grove, Illinois 60515: InterVarsity Press, 1989.

Coger, Marian. *Women in Parish Ministry: Stress and Support.* The Alban Institute, Inc., 1991.

Culver, Elsie Thomas. *Women in the World of Religion.* Garden City, New York: Doubleday & Company Inc., 1967.

Daly, Mary. *Beyond God the Father: Toward a Philosophy of Women's Liberation.* Boston: Beacon Press, 1973.

Elizondo, Virgil, and Norbert Greinacher, eds. *Women in a Men's Church.* New York: The Seabury Press, 1980.

Faricy, Robert S. J. *The Lord's Dealing-The Primacy of the Feminine in Christian Spirituality.* New York and New Jersey: Paulist Press, 1988.

Fischer, Clare Benedicks, Betsy Brenneman, and Anne Bennett, eds. *Women in a Strange Land : Search for a New Image.* Philadelphia: Fortress Press, 1975.

Fisher, Helen E. *The First Sex: The Natural Talents of Women and How They Are Changing the World.* New York: Random House, 1999.

France, R. T. *Women in the Church's Ministry: A Test Case for Biblical Interpretation.* Grand Rapids, Michigan: William B. Eerdmans Publishing Company, 1997.

Gage, Matilda Joslyn. *Woman, Church and State.* New York: Arno Press, 1972.

Grenz, Stanley J., with Denise Muir Kjesbo. *Women in the Church : A Biblical Theology Of Women in Ministry.* Downers Grove, Illinois: InterVarsity Press, 1995.

Hageman, Alice L. ed. *Sexist Religion and Women in the Church : No More Silence!* New York: Association Press, 1974.

Hamilton, Kenneth and Alice. *To be a Man, to Be a Woman.* Nashville and New York: Abingdon Press, 1972.

Holloway, Richard., ed. *Who Needs Feminism? Male Response to Sexism in the Church.* Great Britain: SPCK, 1991.

Irwin, Joyce L., ed. *Anna Maria van Schurman: Whether a Christian Woman Should be Educated and Other Writings from Her Intellectual Circle*. Chicago and London: The University of Chicago Press, 1998.

Jackson, Eleanor, ed. *The Question of a Woman: The Collected Writings of Charlotte Von Kirschbaum*. Grand Rapids, Michigan: Cambridge, UK: William B. Eerdmans Publishing Company, 1996.

Jones, Curtis G. *The Naked Shepherd*. United States of America: Word Books, 1979.

King, Ursula. *Women and Spirituality*. Second edition, Pennsylvania: The Pennsylvania State University Press, University Park, 1993.

Kroeger, Richard Clark and Catherine Clark Kroeger. *I Suffer Not a Woman: Rethinking 1 Timothy 2:11–15 in Light of Ancient Evidence*. Grand Rapids, Michigan: Baker Book House, 1992.

Langley, Myrtle. *Equal Woman: A Christian Feminine Perspective*. Great Britain: Marshall, Morgan & Scott, 1983.

Lewis Boonprasat, Nantawan, Lydia Hernandez, Helen Locklear, and Robina Marie Winbush. *Sisters Struggling in the Spirit: A Woman of Color Theological Anthology*. USA: Women Ministries Program Area, National Ministries Division, Presbyterian Church, 1994.

Lockyer, Herbert. *All the Doctrines of the Bible: A Study Analysis of Major Bible Doctrines*. Grand Rapids, Michigan: Zondervan Publishing House, 1964.

MacArthur, John, Jr. *God's Higher Calling for Women – 1 Timothy 2:9–15*. Chicago: Moody Press, 1987.

McClung, Nellie L. *In Times Like These*. Toronto and Buffalo: University of Toronto Press, 1974.

McGrath, Sister Albertus Magnus, OP. *Women and the Church*. Garden City, New York: Image Books, 1976.

Mitchell, Ella Pearson, ed. *Women – To Preach or Not To Preach: 21 Outstanding Black Preachers Say Yes!* Valley Forge, PA: Judson Press, 1993.

Mollenkott, Virginia Ramsey. *Women, Men and the Bible*. Revised Ed. New York: Crossroad, 1985.

Nardo, Don. *The Rise of Christianity*. P.O. Box v289011, San Diego, CA 92198-9011: Lucent Books, 2001.

Olsen, V. Norkov. *The New Relatedness for Woman & Man in Christ : A Mirror of the

Divine. Loma Linda, California: Loma Linda University, Center for Christian Bioethics, 1993.

Pape, Dorothy R. *In Search of God's Total Ideal Woman: A Personal Examination of the New Testament*. Downers Grove, Illinois 60515: InterVarsity Press, 1977

Porthouse, Clive. ed. *Ministry in the Seventies*, London: Falcon Books, 1970.

Power, Kim. *Veiled Desire: Augustine on Women*. New York: The Continuum Publishing Company, 1996.

Reuther, Rosemary Radford. *Sexism and God Talk: Toward a Feminist Theology*. Boston: Beacon Press, 1983.

Robins, Wendy S. ed. *Through the Eyes of a Woman: Bible Studies on the Experience of Women*. Revised Ed., Switzerland: WCC Publications, World Council of Churches, 150 route de Ferney, 1211 Geneva 2 , Swit., 1995.

Schmidt, Alvin John. *Veiled and Silence: How Culture Shaped Sexist Theology*. Georgia 31207: Mercer University Press, 1990.

Spencer, Aida Besancon. *Beyond the Curse: Women Called to Ministry*. Nashville, Camden, New York: Thomas Nelson Publishers, 1985.

Stuart, Elizabeth and Adrian Thatcher. eds. *Christian Perspectives on Sexuality and Gender*. Broughton Gifford, Wiltshire: The Cromwell Press, 1996.

Swidler, Leonard. *Biblical Affirmations of Woman*. Philadelphia: The Westminster Press, 1979.

Tamez, Elsa. ed. *Through Her Eyes: Women's Theology From Latin America*. Maryknoll, New York: Orbis Books, 1989.

The Berkshire Clergywomen and Alison Stokes. *Women Pastors*. New York: Crossroad, 1995.

Thurston, Bonnie. *Women in the New Testament: Questions and Commentary*. New York: The Crossroad Publishing Company, 1998.

Turabian, Kate. *A Manual for Writers of Term Papers, Theses and Dissertations*. Sixthth ed. Chicago and London: The University of Chicago Press, 1996.

Van Vuren, Nancy. *The Subservience of Women as Practised by Churches, Witch-Hunters, and Other Sexists*. Philadelphia: The Westminster Press, 1974.

Webster, John C. B. and Ellen Low Webster, *The Church and Women in the Third World*, Philadelphia: The Westminster Press, 1985.

Witherington, Ann. ed. *Women and the Genesis of Christianity.* Cambridge: Cambridge University Press, 1992.

Witherington, Ben III. *Women in the Ministry of Jesus – A Study of Jesus' Attitude to Women and Their Role as Reflected in His Early Life.* Cambridge, London, New York, New Rochelle, Melbourne, Sydney: Cambridge University Press, 1984.

Electronic Encyclopedia

Wikipedia the Free Encyclopedia

Electronic Journals Articles

Jungkuntz, Theodore. "Authority – A Charismatic Perspective." *Currents in Theology and Mission* (June 1976): Vol. 3, No. 3: 171–176.

Kanyoro, Musimbi. "Sitting Down Together." *OtherSide* 34 (May–June 1998): 36–39.

Electronic Magazines

Kraft, Marguerite and Meg Crossman. "Women in Missions." *Mission Frontiers* (August 1999): Vol. 21, No. 5–8.

Love, Fran. "Blessing Women in Missions." *Mission Frontiers* (August 1999): Vol. 21, No. 5–8.

Lutz, Lorry. "The AD 2000 Women's Track – Mobilizing Women around the World." *Mission Frontiers* (August 1999): Vol. 21, No. 5–8.

Tucker, Ruth. "Lottie Moon: "Saint" of the Southern Baptists." *Mission Frontier* (August 1999): Vol. 21, No. 5–8.

Reports

"Christian Women of Africa Share in Responsibility." *Report on the Responsibility of Christian Women in Africa Today:* held at Makere University, Kampala, Uganda: April 11–19, 1963. Published jointly by the All African Conference and the Dept. of Cooperation of Men and Women in Church, Family and Society of the World Council of Churches.

Parvey, Conctance F., ed. *The Community of Men and Women in the Church.* Geneva: World Council of Churches, 1983.

"We Listened Long Before We Spoke: A Consultation of the Sub-Unit on Women in Church and Society of the World Council of Churches." n.d., n.p.

Internet (World Wide Web)

_____. "The Male-Only Priesthood Is Not Revealed Truth." [Online] Available SF Bay Catholic Electronic Magazine, mailed November 28, 1995.

_____. "The Roman Catholic Church Has the Authority to Ordain Women." [Online]

Available SF Bay Catholic Electronic Magazine, mailed January 4, 1996.

Andrews, William L. "Julia A. J. Foote (1823–1900)." [Online] Available http://college.hmco.com/English/lauter/heath/4e/student/author_pages/late_nineteenth/ foot, April 11, 2003.

Bowman, Ann L. "Women in Ministry: An Exegetical Study of 1 Timothy 2:11–15." [Online] Available http//www.leaderu.com/isot/docs/womenmin.html, From International School of Theology, Spring 1992.

Christus Victor Ministries. "Women in Ministry, Christianity & Culture." [Online] Available http://www.greghoyd.org/gbfront/index.asp?PageID-282, April 22,2001.

Creflo and Taffi Dollar – Christian Author Profile. [Online} Available http://www.faithcenteredresources.com/authors/creflo-taffi-dollar.asp, April 1, 2003.

Dr. Creflo A. Dollar and his wife, Pastor Taffi Dollar. [Online] Available http://www.cfaith.com/Cfaith/SUPPORT/biography affiliate/0.3909.109.00.asp. April 1, 2003.

Graeme's Home Page. A Theological and Biblical Exposition of the Role of Women and Their Relationship to Men within the Church, with special reference to authority and teaching. [Online] Available http://www.youth.co.za/papers/wommin.htm, April 22, 2003.

Grenz: Theological Foundations for Women in Ministry. [Online] Available http://www.liberty.edu/courses/theo250/grenz.html, April 22, 2001.

Groothuis, Douglas R. and Rebecca Merrill Groothuis. "Southern Baptists and the Subordination of Women." [Online] Available http://www.gospelcom.net/ivpress/groothuis/SBCsubordination.htm, April 3, 2001.

Gutierrez, Luis T. Brothers and Sisters in Christ. [Online] Available S F Bay Catholic Electronic Magazine, mailed October 1996.

Harrison House: About Kenneth and Gloria Copeland. [Online] Available http://www.harrisonhouse.com/AuthorInfo.asp?IDA-621, April 1, 2003.

Hunt, Keith. "Women's Responsibility in the Church-Study No. 3." [Online] Available http;//www.giveshare.org/BibleStudy/003.women.html, May 14, 2004.

Irvin, Charles E. "The Ordination of Women." [Online] Available http://www.re.net/Lansing/st-mary/essays/ordwomen.html, San Francisco Bay Catholic External Report, November 24, 2000.

John Mark Ministries. "Women and Ministry: A Sermon." [Online] Available http://www.Pastornet.net.au/jmm/alpt/alpt0097.htm, April 3, 2001.

Johns, Loren L. "Women in Ministry According to the New Testament: An Exegetical and Theological Issue." [Online] Available http://www.ambs.edu/Ljohns/women.htm, April 22, 2001.

"Joyce Meyer." [Online] Available http://www.twbookmark.com/authors/20/2594/. April 1, 2003.

"Kay Arthur." [Online] Available www.precept.org/about.html, April 1, 2003.

"Kay Arthur – Cofounder of Precept Ministries International." [Online] Available www.preceptflorida.org/Kayarthur.htm, April 1, 2003.

Laing, David (ed.) Selected Writings of John Knox: Public Epistles, Treaties, and Expositions to the Year 1559, Edinburgh 1864. "The First Blast of the Trumpet" By John Knox. [Online] Available www.womenpriests.org

Laird, Rebecca. A Brief Theology of Women in Ministry: Four Reasons Women Should Teach, Preach, and Minister. [Online] Available http://www.messiah.edu/whwc/articles/article32.htm (Spring 1992), April 22, 2001.

Lindsay Roberts. [Online] Available www.orm.cc/bio_lr.html, April 1, 2003.

"Marriage and Women." [Online] Available http://members.aol.com/patriarchy/Gen24/rushVII-3.htm, May 13, 2004.

Melick, Richard R. Jr., PhD. "Women Pastors: What Does the Bible Teach." May 1998 [Online] Available http://www.baptist2baptist.com/b2article.asp?ID=229, May 13, 2004.

Miller, Betty. "What Does the Bible Say about Women in Ministry?" [Online] Available http://www.bible.com/answers/awomenin.html, April 22, 2001.

Pastor Paula White Biography. [Online] Available www.honeybzz4u.com/Events/Paula_White/Paula_white.html, April 1, 2003.

"Pat Francis Biography." [Online] Available http://www.patfrancis.org/biography.htm. April 1, 2003.

"Policy on Women in Ministry – A Biblical and Theological Basis for Women in Ministry." [Online] Available http://www.covchurch.org/cov/html/women_in_min.html, Covenant Publications, 3200W Foster Avenue, Chicago, Illinois, 60625, April 22, 2001.

Ramming, Ida. "The Diaconate – A Ministry for Women in the Church." [Online] Available www.womenpriests.org, from Orientierung 62 91998, pp. 8–11.

Riss, Richard. "A Brief History of Some Women in Ministry." [Online] Available http://www.bible.com/answers/awomenin.html, April 22, 2001.

"Role of Women in the Church 1 Corinthians 11: 1–16." [Online] Available http://www.angelfire.com/nt/theology/1cr11-01.html, 1, May 14, 2004.

Rushmore, Louise. "The Role of Women in the Church." [Online] Available http://www.hope-of-israel.org/woman.htm, Hope of Israel Ministries (Church of YEHOVAH), May 14, 2004.

Sanders, Cheryl J. "History of Women in the Pentecostal Movement." 1996 PCCNA National Conference, Memphis Tennessee, October 1, 1996. [Online] Available http://www.fullnet.net/np/archives/cyberj/sanders.html, April 22, 2001.

Schneiders, Sandra M. "The Effects of Women's Experience on their Spirituality." [Online] Available Spirituality Today, Summer 1983, Vol. 35, No. 2, pp. 100–116.

Spake, Kluane Dr. Submission and Equality – Part III. [Online] Available http://www.womanorfthelasthour.com/new/SUBMISSION%20III.htm

The Place of Women. [Online] Available http://www.pursuingthetruth.org/studies/files/placeofwomen.htm, from A Scriptural Perspective on the Place of Women, © 2000 by William R. Cunningham, Second Edition: February 7, 2001.

The Priesthood of All the Faithful. [Online] Available www.womenpriests.org, from "Did Christ rule out Women priests?" by John Wijngaards, McCrimmon's Great Wakering 1986, pp. 64–68.

The Role of Women in Ministry. [Online] Available www.ag.org/top/position-papare/4191-women-ministry.cfm, April 22, 2001.

Wijngaards, John. When Women were deacons. [Online] Available www.womenpriests.org, The Tablet, May 8, 1999, pp. 623–624.

Without Walls International Church. [Online] Available www.withoutwalls.org/pastor.htm, April 1, 2003.

Women in Ministry – A Study Paper for New York Mennonite Conference. [Online] Available http://freenet.buffalo.edu/-nymennon/womenmin.htm, April 24, 2001.

Women Priests in the Anglican Community. [Online] Available www.religioustolerance.com, April 1, 2001.

Zikmund, Barbara Brown, Adair T. Lummis and Patricia M. Y. Chang. "Women, Men and Styles of Clergy Leadership." [Online] Available wysiwyg//35/http://hirrhartaem.edu/bookshelf/clergywomen_summary.html. April 1, 2001.

Index

Symbols

1 Timothy 2:11–15 34–36, 52, 153, 156

A

Aaron 56, 57
Acorn to Youth Services. *See* Francis, Pat
Adam 7, 9–11, 13, 15, 23, 35, 36, 38, 42, 49, 140, 141
administrative component 137, 138
African Regional Consultation 24
Alexander the Great 15
American Baptist Church 82
Anglican Churches 39, 86, 118
apostle, definition of 63
Apostolic Constitutions 67, 114
Apostolic Faith Church. *See* Open Bible Standard
Aquinas. *See* Thomas Aquinas, Saint
Areopagus 14
Aristotle 12, 13, 15, 21, 23, 27
Armstrong, Annie 104
Arrow Records 100
Arthur, Kay 100, 110, 157
asceticism 6, 66. *See also* Stoic philosophy
Athaliah (queen) 60
Athenian women 16
Augustine, Saint 13
Aylward, Gladys 106

B

Barak (warrior) 58. *See also* Deborah
Barot, Madeleine 108
Bebel, August 108
   Die frau und der sozialismus 108
Bethel 58
Bible 3, 4, 7, 21, 25, 32, 37, 38, 53, 55, 57, 69, 75, 77, 80, 82, 86, 90, 93, 94, 97, 99–101, 105, 109, 122, 153, 154, 157, 158, 169, 170
Bjerkas, Ingrid 85
black woman leaders. *See* Lee, Jarena; Elaw, Zilpha; Foote, Julia
Blandina (slave girl) 22, 117
Bliss, Kathleen 108
Book of Decrees (Gratian) 117
Booth, Catherine 95
Booth, William 95
Bright, Bill 104
Brown, Antoinette 82, 93
Brunner, Emil 15, 26

C

Calvin, John 23
Campus Crusade for Christ. *See* Bright, Bill
Canham, Elizabeth 118, 127
   Pilgrimage to Priesthood 118
canon law 117, 118
Carmichael, Amy 105, 111

Catherine of Siena 91
celibacy 6, 15, 93, 104, 117
Chalcedon, Council of 67
charismatic component 138, 146, 148
charismatic phase 122
Charlotte von Kirschbaum 52, 108, 153
   Die wirkliche frau 108
Christianity 1, 8, 16, 17, 19, 20, 46, 62, 69, 72, 117, 118, 142, 147, 153, 155, 156
Christian Revival Association. *See* Booth, Catherine
Clement of Alexandria 7, 13
clericalism 144
Compassion for the Poor 102. *See also* Francis, Pat
competitive power 46
Congregationalists 39, 82, 83, 94, 95, 96. *See also* United Church of Christ
Conservative Baptist Association 88
Constantine xv, 22, 170
Constantinople, Council of 67
contemporary women's movement 107
Copeland, Gloria 100, 101, 110, 157
courtesans 12
Crawford, Florence L. 98
Creation Theory 2, 8, 141
credential phase 122

D

Daily Blessing: Make Your Day Count 101
deacon 30, 39, 66–69, 71, 83, 85, 86, 97, 138, 158
deaconesses 64, 66–68, 85, 114–116
   decline of the 68
   office of 67, 113
Deaconess Movement 92, 93
Deaconess, Order of 68, 114, 115
Deborah 57, 58, 60, 86
Decretals 117
Decretum Gratiani (Gratiani) 117
Die frau und der sozialismus (Bebel) 108
Die wirkliche frau (Kirschbaum) 108
discrimination 61, 113, 115, 119–121, 138, 142, 146

divorce 6, 14, 16–18, 56, 83, 141
Dohnavur Fellowship 106, 111
Dollar, Taffi 100, 110, 156
Dones de Reyes, Luz M. 106
Dow, Betsy 84
Dowdy, Naomi 106

E

Eagle Mountain International Church. *See* Kenneth Copeland Ministries
economic subordination 4
egalitarianism 92, 134, 147
Egalitarians 9, 21, 41, 47, 122
Egyptian women 16
Elaw, Zilpha 97, 98
Elect Lady 64
Elliot, Elizabeth 107
England, Church of 85, 86, 89
Epaon, Council of 68
Epiphanus (bishop of Salamis) 7
equality xix, 2, 4, 7–10, 17, 20–24, 27, 39, 41, 43, 49, 69, 80, 83, 86, 93, 94, 105, 115, 138, 140, 142, 145, 147, 151, 158. *See also* subordination: organizational
Esther (queen) 59, 60, 81
Eucharist 30, 31, 39, 78, 87, 89, 126, 145. *See also* women leaders
Euodia 63
Eve 7, 9–11, 13, 15, 23, 35, 36, 38, 42, 44, 49, 140, 141
exploitative power 46

F

Fabiola 22
fall, effects of the 140, 141, 142
false teaching 34–36, 35
fear, godly 114
Felicity 22
Fell, Margaret 91
female xiii, xviii, 5, 6, 9, 10, 12–14, 18–24, 26, 27, 30–33, 35, 39, 42, 45, 47–51, 55, 56, 62, 64–67, 72, 74–78, 80, 84, 85, 88, 89, 91, 92, 94,

98, 104–106, 108, 111, 114–116, 120–125, 129, 132–134, 137, 139, 140, 142, 143, 146–148, 170
female leaders xviii, 5, 30, 49, 123, 125, 129, 139, 146
female leadership 120, 122, 123, 129, 134
fetal development. *See* inferiority myth: biological
Florence Li Tim-Oi 86
Foote, Julia 97
Francis, Pat 100, 102, 110, 158
Franson, Fredrick 103, 104, 105
Freewill Baptists 88, 95
Fundamentalist churches 82

G

Galatians 3:28 20, 21, 23, 27, 79, 80, 82, 86, 142. *See also* egalitarianism; equality
General Assembly of Massachusetts 82
General Association of Congregational Ministers of Massachusetts 94
Genesis 3:16 1, 7, 23, 37, 42. *See also* subordination
Germany, women from 92
God
    gender of 78
    nature of. *See* Nicene Creed
godly 2, 8, 11, 35, 114
God the Father 2, 3, 32, 40, 51, 78, 152
Gratian
    Book of Decrees 117
Gratiani
    Decretum Gratiani 117
Greece, ancient 5, 12
Greek culture 15, 36
Greek Orthodox Church 87
Grimké, Angelina 81, 93
Grimké, Sarah 93, 94
    "Letters on the Equality of the Sexes and the Conditions of Women" 94

H

Halverson, Richard 104
harrasment, coping strategies against 121
Hastings, Selina 91
headship 8, 9, 40–43, 45, 61
Hebrew culture 6, 14
Heck, Barbara 91
Helena (Constantine's mother) 22
He Loves Me, He Loves Me Not (White) 101
Hoch, Dorothee 108
    Weg und aufgabe der frau heute 108
Holy Ghost xviii, 3, 72
Holy Spirit xv, xvii, xviii, 9, 30, 32, 37, 40, 44, 46–50, 67, 71, 72, 74, 75, 76, 80, 82, 87, 97, 107, 109, 114, 137, 138, 143, 146, 148, 170
Huldah (prophetess) 57, 59
Hutchinson, Anne 91

I

inferiority myth 12
    biological 13
    intellectual 13, 14
    social 14
    spiritual 2, 14
integrative power 46, 47
Irvin, Charles E. 87, 90, 157
Isidore (archbishop) 15

J

Jesus Christ xvii, xviii, 2–4, 11, 15, 17–20, 24, 29–32, 37, 39, 40, 42–44, 45–51, 60, 61, 65, 68, 73, 74, 77–79, 87, 94, 96, 98, 101, 126, 138, 139, 142, 143, 145, 147, 148, 170
    male priests and 31
    submission of 3, 48, 51
Jewish culture 5, 6
Joanna (wife of Chuza) 18
job shortages 120
John Paul II 87
    Ordinatio sacerdotalis 87
Josephus (historian) 13

Josiah (king) 59
Judaism 1, 16, 17, 64
judges 55, 57, 58
Judith 59

K

Kenneth Copeland Ministries 101, 110
kephale, definition of 41
Kingdom Covenant Ministries.
    See Francis, Pat
Kuhlman, Kathryn 99

L

Laodicea, Council of 65, 114
laying on of hands. See ordination
leadership xvii, xviii, xix, 3, 17, 21, 24, 26, 27, 29, 30, 32–34, 37, 41, 43–48, 50–53, 55, 57–64, 68, 69, 71, 73–75, 76, 78, 83, 88, 90–93, 96, 97, 99, 105, 107, 115–118, 120, 122–124, 127, 129–135, 138, 143–145, 151, 159, 169
leadership style 44, 47, 129, 130, 132, 134, 135
Lee, Jarena 97, 98
Lee, Luther 82
"Letters on the Equality of the Sexes and the Conditions of Women" (Grimké) 94
Lewis, Jesse Penn 99
Life in the Word Inc. 100
Lord's Supper. See Eucharist
Lutheran Church 82, 85
Luther, Martin 13, 23, 26, 117
Lydia 62, 64, 153

M

male authority xviii, 30, 71, 75
male domination 23, 24, 32, 33, 42, 45, 52, 69, 116, 122, 126, 142, 146, 147
male leadership xviii, 3, 26, 33, 48, 50, 58, 76, 90, 92, 120, 123, 130
Mallet, Sarah 92
manipulative power 46

marginalization xvii, xviii, 113, 114, 118, 122, 123, 126, 146
marriage 6, 8, 10, 16–18, 21, 23, 27, 38, 41, 42, 56, 69, 76–78, 92, 105, 140, 151, 157
Martha 18
martyrs, female. See Blandina; Felicity; Perpetua
Mary 18, 63, 64, 90, 94, 98, 99, 107, 127, 133, 135, 150, 152, 157
Mary Magdalene 18
McPherson, Aimee Semple 95, 96, 99
Mears, Henrietta 104
Methodist Church 82, 84, 85
Meyer, Joyce 100, 110, 157
ministry xi, xiii, xv, xvii, xviii, xix, 3–5, 14, 18, 21, 25–27, 29–31, 36–40, 43, 44, 46, 49, 50, 52, 53, 55, 58, 60–62, 64, 66–69, 72–76, 78, 80–86, 88, 89, 91, 93, 95–100, 101–107, 109–111, 113–127, 129, 131–135, 137–139, 142–152, 154–159, 169–171
Miracles Now 101
Miriam (prophetess) 57, 60
Moe, Malla 105
Monsen, Marie 106
Montgomery, Carrie Judd 95, 96
Montgomery, Helen Barret 104
Moody, D. L. 84, 103–105. See also Moe, Malla; Willard, Frances
Moon, Charlotte Diggs 105
Moore, Esther 81
Mosaic law 17, 18
Moschella, Betty Clark 124
Mott, Lucretia 81
mutual dependence 9, 50, 51
mutual destruction 51
Mutual Submissive model 47, 50, 51

N

New Creation theory 141
New York Mennonite Conference 43, 53, 159. See also Women in Ministry
Nicene Creed 3

Noadiah (prophetess) 59
North American Baptist Conference 88
nutrient power 46

O

Oliver, Anna 84
Olympia Brown 83
Open Bible Standard 99
Orange, Council of 68
Orange, Synod of 67
Order of Creation Theory 8
Order of Widows 64, 65, 66, 113
ordination 27, 30, 31, 37–39, 66–68, 71–90, 95, 120, 122, 125, 157
  of women 27, 38, 39, 67, 71, 75, 77–83, 85–90, 125, 157
Ordinatio Sacerdotalis (John Paul II) 87
Orleans, Council of 67, 68
Orthodox churches 82, 87
Orthodox Congregational 81
Oswald, Roy 134

P

Palmer, Phoebe 95, 96
Parker, Mary 94
participatory management 130. *See also* leadership style
partnership style 132, 134
pastoral widows 66
patriarchy 1, 3, 22, 49, 50, 143–147, 157
Perpetua 22, 117
Pharisees 15, 18, 20
Philo (scholar) 13
Phoebe 63, 86, 95, 96
Pilgrimage to Priesthood (Canham) 118, 127
Plato 12, 13
Polycarp 66
power xviii, 1, 2, 6, 11, 17, 24, 29, 32, 37, 44–46, 47, 49, 53, 81, 82, 94, 95, 98, 102, 104, 107, 109, 114, 116, 124, 130–133, 137, 139, 140, 144, 145, 147, 154, 170
powerlessness 46

preaching 35, 64, 72, 79–82, 84, 92, 95, 97–99, 102, 103, 107, 117, 132
Precept Ministries International 100, 101, 110, 157
presbyter 65, 67, 114. *See also* woman presbyter
Presbyterian Church 53, 82, 85, 104, 110, 153
Prestige Ministry 100
priesthood 31, 32, 39, 56, 61, 71–78, 79, 80, 86–90, 113–116, 118, 127, 149, 156, 158. *See also* male domination
priesthood of believers 31, 32, 39, 73, 75, 76, 79, 80
Priscilla 62, 63, 143
prophetesses 36, 55, 57, 57–59, 65, 170
prostitutes 12, 56, 120
Protestantism 31, 93

Q

Quakers 39, 91, 93, 95, 96
queens 55, 60

R

Rees, Seth Cook 95, 96
Reformed Church 39, 108
reincarnation 12
respectability, full institutional 122, 123
Roberts, Lindsay 100, 101, 110, 157
Roman Catholic Church 31, 83, 87, 156
Roman culture 6, 7, 14, 17
Ruth 59, 60, 99, 111, 155

S

salary 33, 104, 113, 119. *See also* discrimination
Salome Alexandra 60
Salvation Army 39, 96. *See also* Booth, Catherine
Samaritan woman, Jesus and the 18, 19
sanctification, doctrine of 97
servanthood xviii, 29, 30, 32, 33, 118, 138, 139
servant leadership 29, 30

sexual harassment 113, 120, 121
sexual intimacy 6, 22, 23
shared leadership 96, 131
slavery 33, 34, 81, 93, 94
Slessor, Mary 107
Smith, Amanda 84. *See also* Oliver, Anna
Snowden, Anna. *See* Oliver, Anna
Socrates 12
Southern Baptist Convention 88
South Tampa Christian Center 101. *See also* Without Walls International Church
Sparta, women of 16
Stoic philosophy 6
stress 6, 8, 11, 33, 35, 40, 49, 78, 129, 134, 135, 152
Strong, R. A. 83
submission 1–5, 8, 29, 34, 35, 40, 41, 46–51, 53, 76, 78, 140, 158
submission model 47–50
subordination xviii, 1–4, 5–8, 12, 17, 23, 24, 33, 48, 49, 64, 83, 137–141, 156
   female xviii, 24, 49
   godly 2
   organizational 4
   ungodly 2, 3
subordination myth 5
superiority 4, 5, 7, 8, 10, 145
Suzanna 18
Synod of Orange 67
Syntyche 63

T

Tabitha 65
Taylor, Hudson 103, 104
teachers 25, 34–38, 61, 72, 77, 79, 80, 91, 103, 107, 122
teaching, false 34, 35, 36
temperance movement 93
teshuqa, definition of 7
Testamentum Domini Nostri Jesu Christi 66
Thomas Aquinas, Saint 13, 15, 23, 27, 31
Torah, women and 16, 18, 38, 56

Transform Student Ministries 101. *See also* Arthur, Kay
Transubstantiation, Doctrine of 31
Trevecca House 92. *See also* Hastings, Selina

U

United Church of Christ 82, 83, 132
Ure, Betty 124, 127

V

Vatican Declaration on the Ordination of Women 87
verbal harassment 121
vestal virgins 16

W

Walling, William H. 14
water baptism xvii, 20
Webster-Smith, Irene 106
Weg und aufgabe der frau heute (Hoch) 108
Wesley, John 92
White, Paula 100, 101, 110, 157
   He Loves Me, He Loves Me Not 101
widows 62, 64–68, 71, 72, 113, 114, 116. *See also* Order of Widows; pastoral widows; woman presbyters
Willard, Frances 84, 93, 103
   Women in the Pulpit 84
Witherington, Ben 21, 27, 69, 155
Without Walls International Church 101, 102, 110, 158
wives xi, 1, 5, 6, 8, 10–12, 14, 17, 18, 21, 23, 35, 37, 38, 40–42, 47–49, 51, 55, 56, 63, 76, 77, 104, 106, 110, 119, 120, 156
women xi, xiii, xv, xvii, xviii, xix, 1–27, 29–53, 55–69, 71, 72, 74–111, 113–127, 129–135, 137–159, 169–171
   as objects of sexuality 15
   as public reformers 94
   as teachers 36, 91

Athenian view of 5, 6, 13, 16
"Women in Ministry" 43
"Women in the Pulpit" (Willard) 84
women leaders xi, xiii, xvii, xviii, xix, 3, 17, 24, 30, 31, 55, 60–64, 79, 83, 86, 91, 93, 96–98, 100, 102, 104, 106, 107, 113, 115, 117, 119, 122–126, 129–132, 134, 137, 139, 141, 145–147, 149, 169
   future of 145
   invisibility of 123
   marginalization of 122, 126
   silence of 123
   traditional roles and 77
women presbyters 65. *See also* widows
Women's Christian Temperance Union (WCTU) 93
Women's Ministry 100
Women's Union Missionary Society 103
Woodworth-Etier, Maria B. 95
World Changers Church International 100

Testimonials:

It was with great zeal that I read this book and I am now richer in my understanding of its subject. The availability of the book has been rightly timed. It is exciting, educative, insightful, well-written and a work of excellence. I strongly advocate that it be embraced by both men and women as a welcome addition to their libraries. I believe that this book will be a source of great encouragement for women in ministry, as well as a good reason for their further acceptance and advancement in the service of the Lord.

Waveney E. Job

• •

I felt privileged to read the manuscript of the book *Women Leaders in Ministry: From Bondage to Freedom at Last!* This book is an inspiration for women who are in leadership, to take them to another level. In a culture characterized by so much suppression of women leaders, the book is an eye-opener for all women.

I was encouraged and inspired to continue to fulfill my call to spiritual leadership.

Reverend M. Janet Thompson

• •

This book is a joy to read. Throughout history, men have taken upon themselves to be biased about women in ministry. This book brings out pointers regarding women who have been used by God in Old Testament, New Testament and contemporary times. The Bible declares that we are joint-heirs (both male and female) with Christ, to be used for His glory. Throughout the ages, women have been deterred from taking their rightful places in the body of Christ. Jesus Christ has declared that He will build His church and the gates of hell shall not prevail against it.

Barbara Cain

....

When I read the manuscript of this book, I became fully convinced that women should be allowed to play a significant role in ministry. I am not saying that you the readers should agree with me, but after you read the book, your eyes will be opened to the truth that it reveals regarding women in ministry. In today's society, there are man-made views on how women should act and what roles they should perform in the church. I believe that as men, we have forgotten that there were prophetesses in Old and New Testament times. This book has highlighted the names and roles of several prominent women in the bible.

It is time that male leaders take heed and understand that women are a valuable part of the ministry and of the body of Christ. I understand how some men feel about women preachers. However, in 1 Timothy 2:11-14, Paul specifically admonished the Ephesian women of his day. He did not specify that women should not participate in the five-fold ministry. In 1 Corinthians 12, the bible reveals that there are diversities of gifts and operations. God has given the author the insight to write this book to enlighten its readers to the fact the God imparts gifts to both men and women, and equips them to do His work. I encourage you the readers to embrace this book with open minds.

Reverend Gordon Constantine

....

This book challenges evangelical frameworks and empowers believers, and non-believers alike, to rethink and redefine the practical application of the limitless power of the Holy Spirit in the life of a servant of God, irrespective of gender.

It is an exceptional work that continues to demonstrate the need to renew the mind as it relates to a biblical view of ministry standards, practices and realities that oppressive thinking needs to be purged from the body of Christ.

The book captures modern day biases, then stimulates the mind of the reader to search for solutions to work towards the eradication of gender barriers in today's churches. It is wonderfully written with distinct clarity, insight and understanding of the struggles that women face in ministry.

It provides modern day dialogue to consider, and addresses and inspires its readers to examine practical kingdom perspectives as they relate to gender, to the call of God on our lives, and to how we respond to God's servants irrespective of gender or any other humanly defined characteristic. From beginning to end, the author emphasizes the need for the dismantling of carnal thinking in the church.

This book is a "must" read for those who desire to impact their world and change generations.

Joylyn Hewitt
Operational Administrator, Media Department,
Kingdom Covenant Centre.

CPSIA information can be obtained at www.ICGtesting.com
Printed in the USA
LVOW061138091211

258496LV00002B/1/P